50 baby bootees to knit

LITTLE BOOTEES AND SNUGGLY SOCKS
FOR NEWBORN TO NINE MONTHS

Zoë Mellor

COLLINS & BROWN

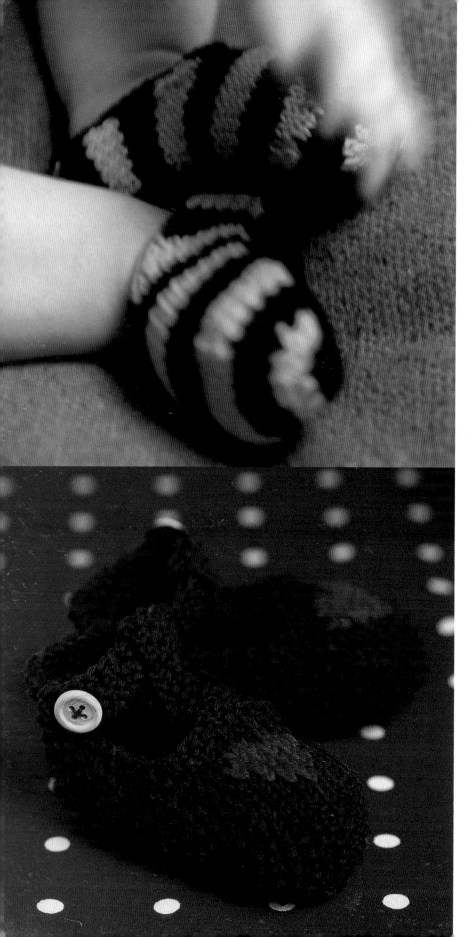

For Toby tiger and Bump, who will be wearing lots of these bootees.

First published in the United Kingdom in 2002
First published in paperback in 2009 by
Collins & Brown
10 Southcombe Street
London
W14 0RA

An imprint of Anova Books Company Ltd

Photography by Joey Toller

ISBN 978-1-84340-507-8

A CIP catalogue for this book is available from the British Library.

10 9 8 7 6 5 4 3 2 1

Reproduction by Rival Colour Ltd, UK
Printed and bound by Imago, Singapore

This book can be ordered direct from the publisher.
Contact the marketing department, but try your bookshop first.

www.anovabooks.com

Contents

Knitters will often admit to an unfinished sweater or two, projects abandoned due to lack of time in a busy schedule. A pair of baby bootees, however, are so tiny and quick to knit that they will never be left half-finished. They also offer a great way to use up spare yarn and experiment with interesting colorways.

Being a bit of a shoe hoarder myself, the thought of designing 50 pairs of bootees and socks was a wonderful challenge. I have done some fun, modern designs to add a special touch to a tiny tot's tootsies and bring a smile to everyone's face. Also, I have designed some more traditional bootees in contemporary colorways to give them fresh appeal and cater for everyone's needs and tastes.

My favorites are the ladybird shoes (page 74) and the fuchsia-pink ribbon-tie bootees (page 114). The bunny and bear bootees (page 52) are very popular with customers in my shop. The jester bootees with bells (page 66) are fabulous for Christmas babies, as they jingle whenever your little one wriggles. All of the bootees make fantastic gifts and great keepsakes.

This book has been a real delight to do and with so many styles to choose from there's no excuse not to knit at least one pair. Go on, get those needles out and make all those little toes snug and warm!

Happy knitting.

Zoë Mellor

fair isle and frill bootees

Pretty pastel bootees for special occasions, the frilled top is very effective, and very easy to knit. These bootees look great in bright colors as well as pastels.

SIZE
To fit baby of 6–9 months

MATERIALS
Rowan true 4 ply botany
1¾oz (50g) balls each of
    pink (M)   1
    cream (C)   1
Small amounts of mauve (A)
    and yellow (B)
1 pair of US 2 (3mm) needles
39in (100cm) of ribbon

BEFORE YOU START
Gauge (Tension)
28sts and 38 rows = 4in (10cm)
square over stockinette (stocking)
stitch using US 2 (3mm) needles.

Abbreviations
See page 126.

BASIC KNIT
Cuff
Using C, cast on 122sts and
knit 1 row.
ROW 2: p1, [*p3tog* three times,
p2] to end.
ROW 3: using M, *k2tog* twice,
k3, k2tog nine times, k3,
k2tog twice. (43sts)
Change to stockinette (stocking)
stitch, work 2 rows.
ROW 3: *k2, yo, k2tog* to last
3 sts, k3.
Work 3 more rows.

Divide for top of foot
K29, turn, p15, turn.
On 15sts, work 22 rows.
Break yarn.
With RS facing, (14sts on needle),
rejoin M and pick up 15sts along
side of foot, 15sts from toe, 15sts
along side of foot and 14sts on
needle. (73sts)
ROW 1: knit.
ROW 2: work Fair Isle following
instructions and chart: using
C, knit.
ROW 3: purl *1B, 1C* to last
st, 1B.
ROW 4: using C, knit.
ROW 5: purl, *1A, 3C* to last
st, 1A.
ROW 6: knit *1B, 1A, 1C, 1A* to
last st, 1B.
ROW 7: as row 5.
ROW 8: as row 4.
ROW 9: Using B, dec, purl to last
2sts, dec. Break yarns. (71 sts)

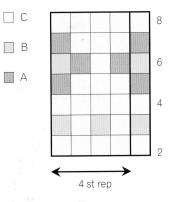

4 st rep

Shape sole
Using M,
ROW 1: k1, *k2tog, k29,
k2tog* k3, *to* again, k1.
ROW 2: k30, k2tog, k3,
k2tog, k30.
ROW 3: k1, *k2tog, k26,
k2tog* k3, *to* again, k1.
ROW 4: k27, k2tog, k3, k2tog, k27.
ROW 5: k1, *k2tog, k23, k2tog*
k3, *to* again, k1.
ROW 6: bind (cast) off.

Second bootee
Make second bootee to match.

FINISHING
Join leg seam and under foot
seam. Weave in any loose
ends. Cut ribbon in half, thread
through eyelets and tie in bow
(see page 123).

textured shoes
A great classic shape, these buttoned shoes are worked in cotton and the simple design shows off the stitch texture well.

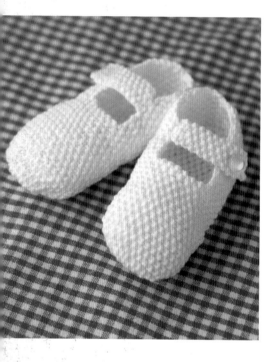

SIZE
To fit baby of 3–6 months

MATERIALS
Rowan 4 ply cotton
1¾oz (50g) ball of
   white   1
1 pair of US 2 (2¾mm) needles
Safety pin
2 small buttons

BEFORE YOU START
Gauge (Tension)
28sts and 38 rows = 4in (10cm) square over stockinette (stocking) stitch using US 2 (2¾mm) needles.

Abbreviations
See page 126.

BASIC KNIT
Sole
Cast on 24sts and work in seed (moss) stitch.
Inc each end of rows 2, 4, 6, and 8. *(32sts)*
Work 3 rows. Dec each end of rows 12, 14, 16 and 18. *(24sts)*
ROW 19: seed (moss) to end, cast on 8sts.

Upper
Inc beg of 2nd and every alt row to 38sts. *(Row 12)*
ROW 13: bind (cast) off 12sts, seed (moss) 3, bind (cast) off 4sts, seed (moss) to end.
ROW 14: seed (moss) 19, leave 3sts on safety pin.
ROWS 15–25: seed (moss) stitch.
ROW 26: seed (moss) 19, cast on 19sts.
ROW 27: seed (moss) stitch.
ROW 28: dec, seed (moss) to end.
ROW 29–38: as rows 27–28.
ROW 39: bind (cast) off.

Strap
Place 3sts from safety pin onto needle.
ROW 1: inc, inc, k1.
ROWS 2–15: seed (moss) stitch.
ROW 16: seed (moss) 2, bind (cast) off 1, seed (moss) 2.
ROW 17: seed (moss) 2, yo, seed (moss) 2.
ROWS 18–20: seed (moss) stitch.
ROW 21: bind (cast) off.

Second shoe
Make second shoe to match.

FINISHING
Join heel seam. Carefully fit upper to sole, easing fullness around toe area, and stitch into position. Seed (moss) stitch is reversible so take care to stitch up second shoe as a mirror image of first shoe, so obtaining a left and a right shoe. Weave in any loose ends. Stitch on buttons (see page 123).

KK352518

cable bootees

These bootees are a very original design with a simple cable winding right around the baby's feet. The cable really stands out when it is knitted in a contrast color, but for a more subtle look you could knit the whole bootee in one color.

SIZE
To fit baby of 0–3(3–6:6–9) months

MATERIALS
Jaeger wool cotton
1¾oz (50g) balls each of
    lilac (A)   1
    cream (B)   1
1 pair of US 3 (3¼mm) needles
Cable needle

BEFORE YOU START
Gauge (Tension)
24sts and 32 rows = 4in (10cm) square over stockinette (stocking) stitch using US 3 (3¼mm) needles.

Abbreviations
c6b = slip 3 sts onto cable needle and hold at back of work, k3 from left hand needle, then k3 from cable needle.
See also page 126.

BASIC KNIT
Cable strip
Using B, cast on 8sts.
ROW 1: knit.
ROW 2: k1, p6, k1.
ROWS 3–4: as rows 1–2.
ROW 5: k1, c6b, k1.
ROW 6: as row 2.
ROWS 7–72(84:96): as rows 1–6 eleven (thirteen:fifteen) times, placing markers at each end of row 37(43:49).
Work rows 1–2 again.
Bind (cast) off.

Sole
Using A, pick up and knit 63(73:83)sts along cable strip, 31(36:41)sts each side of marked row and 1st on marked row.
ROWS 1–3: knit.
ROW 4: k2, *s1, k1, psso, k25(30:35), k2tog* k1, *to* again, k2.
ROW 5: knit.
ROW 6: k2, *s1, k1, psso, k23(28:33), k2tog* k1, *to* again, k2.
ROW 7: knit.
ROW 8: k2, *s1, k1, psso, k21(26:31), k2tog* k1, *to* again, k2.
ROW 9: knit.
ROW 10: bind (cast) off.

Upper
Using B, cast on 32(34:36)sts.
Change to A and knit 1 row. Work 15 rows in k1, p1 rib.
Change to stockinette (stocking) stitch and work 4(6:8) rows.
ROWS 5–6: bind (cast) off 11sts, work to end.
On 10(12:14)sts, work 14(16:18) rows. Bind (cast) off.

Second bootee
Make second bootee to match.

FINISHING
Join sole and heel seam. Join leg seam. Pin center front of upper to center of cable strip. Ease upper shoe to fit round cable strip and stitch into position (see page 123). Weave in any loose ends.

anchor bootees
Neatly nautical, these bootees are great for all little sailors. Warm wool will keep tiny toes warm on the coldest days, at sea or on shore.

SIZE
To fit baby of 3–6 months

MATERIALS
Jaeger merino 4 ply
1¾oz (50g) ball each of
    navy (M)   1
    cream (C)   1
1 pair of US 2 (3mm) needles

BEFORE YOU START
Gauge (Tension)

28sts and 38 rows = 4in (10cm) square over stockinette (stocking) stitch using US 2 (3mm) needles.

Abbreviations
See page 126.

BASIC KNIT
Cuff

Using C, cast on 42sts. Change to M and work 2½in (6cm) in k1, p1 rib, dec end of last row. (41sts) Change to stockinette (stocking) stitch. Work 4 rows.

Divide for top of foot

K28 turn, p15, turn.
On 15sts, work 8 rows.
Row 9: place anchor motif: knit 7M, 1C, 7M.
Work anchor motif then work 4 more rows (toe), break yarn. With RS facing, (13sts on needle), rejoin M and pick up 11sts along side of foot, 15sts from toe, 11sts along side of foot and 13sts on needle. (63sts)
Cont as folls:
ROW 1: using M, knit.
ROWS 2–3: using C, knit.
ROWS 4–5: using M, knit.
ROWS 6–13: as rows 2–5 twice.
Break C.

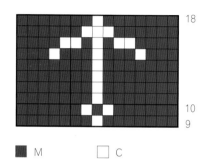

M   C

Shape sole

Using M,

ROW 1: k1, *k2tog, k25, k2tog*
k3, *to* again, k1.

ROW 2: k26, k2tog, k3,
k2tog, k26.

ROW 3: k1, *k2tog, k22, k2tog*
k3, *to* again, k1.

ROW 4: k23, k2tog, k3,
k2tog, k23.

ROW 5: k1, *k2tog, k19, k2tog*
k3, *to* again, k1.

ROW 6: bind (cast) off.

Second bootee

Make second bootee to match.

FINISHING

Join leg seam and under foot
seam (see page 123). Weave in
any loose ends.

simple t-bar shoes

These are a popular design and the t-bar shape means that they can be buttoned onto the liveliest foot with confidence.

simple t-bar shoes cont

SIZE
To fit baby of 6–9 months

MATERIALS
Rowan cotton glacé
1¾oz (50g) ball of
 lilac   1
1 pair of US 3 (3¼mm) needles
Safety pin
2 small buttons

BEFORE YOU START
Gauge (Tension)
24sts and 30 rows = 4in
(10cm) square over stockinette
(stocking) stitch using
US 3 (3¼mm) needles.

Abbreviations
See page 126.

BASIC KNIT
Right shoe
Sole
Cast on 19sts and work in seed
(moss) stitch.
Inc each end of rows 2, 4, and 6.
(25sts)
Work 3 rows. Dec each end of
rows 10, 12 and 14. *(19sts)*
ROW 15: seed (moss) to end,
cast on 6sts.

Upper
ROW 1: knit.
ROW 2: inc, purl to end.
ROWS 3–6: as rows 1–2 twice.
ROW 7: knit.
ROW 8: inc, p10, seed (moss) 17.
ROW 9: seed (moss) 17, k12.
ROW 10: inc, p11, seed (moss) 17.
(30sts)
ROW 11: bind (cast) off 10sts, seed
(moss) 3, bind (cast) off 2sts,
seed (moss) 2, k13.
ROW 12: p13, seed (moss) 2, leave
3sts on safety pin.
ROW 13: seed (moss) 2, k13.
ROWS 14–21: as rows 12–13 four
times, placing markers on rows
16, 17 & 18 at seed (moss)
stitch end.

ROW 22: p13, seed (moss) 2, cast
on 15sts.
ROW 23: seed (moss) 17, k13.
ROW 24: p2tog, p11, seed (moss) 17.
ROW 25: seed (moss) 17, k12.
ROW 26: p2tog, purl to end.
ROWS 27–32: work in stockinette
(stocking) stitch, dec beg of each
purl row. *(25sts)*
ROW 33: bind (cast) off.

Strap A
Place 3sts from safety pin
onto needle.
ROWS 1–15: seed (moss) stitch.
ROW 16: seed (moss) 1, bind (cast)
off 1, seed (moss) 1.
ROW 17: seed (moss) 1, yo, seed
(moss) 1.
ROWS 18–19: seed (moss) stitch.
ROW 20: bind (cast) off.

Strap B
RS facing, pick up 3sts from
marker on rows 16, 17 & 18. Work
20 rows in seed (moss) stitch.
Bind (cast) off.

Left shoe
Sole
As for right shoe.

Upper
Reverse stockinette (stocking)
stitch, eg:
ROW 1: purl.
ROW 2: inc, knit to end.
ROW 8: inc, k10, seed (moss) 17.

FINISHING
Join heel seam. Carefully fit upper
to sole, easing fullness around
toe area, and stitch into position.
Weave in any loose ends. Fold
center strap B over to make a
loop for cross strap A. Stitch
in place. Thread strap A through
loop. Stitch on buttons (see
page 123).

polka-dot socks

Fun and functional, these socks look great in almost any color combination, so they are perfect for using up small quantities of yarns.

SIZE

To fit baby of 3–6 months

MATERIALS

Jaeger merino 4 ply
1¾oz (50g) ball each of
blue (M)   1
cream (C)   1
4 double-ended US 2
(3mm) needles

BEFORE YOU START

Gauge (Tension)

28sts and 38 rows = 4in (10cm) square over stockinette (stocking) stitch using US 2 (3mm) needles.

Abbreviations

See page 126.

BASIC KNIT

Note: place marker at beginning of round.

Cuff

Using M, cast on 32sts (10, 10 and 12sts). Work 3 rounds in *k1, p1* to end.
Change to every round, knit.
ROUND 4: M.
ROUND 5: 2C, 6M.
ROUNDS 6–7: 3C, 4M, 1C.
ROUND 8: as round 5.
ROUND 9: M.
ROUND 10: 4M, 2C, 2M.
ROUNDS 11–12: 3M, 4C, 1M.
ROUND 13: as round 10.
ROUNDS 14–18: as rounds 4–8.

Start heel

ROUND 19: using M, k15 turn, leave remaining sts on needles for instep.
On 15sts, work 7 rows in stockinette (stocking) stitch, starting with a purl row.

Shape heel

ROW 1: k9, turn.
ROW 2: s1, p2, turn.
ROW 3: s1, k1, s1, k1, psso, k1, turn.
ROW 4: s1, p2, p2tog, p1, turn.
ROW 5: s1, k3, s1, k1, psso, k1, turn.
ROW 6: s1, p4, p2tog, p1, turn.
ROW 7: s1, k5, s1, k1, psso, turn.
ROW 8: s1, p6, p2tog, p1.
Break yarn.

Using M, pick up and knit 6sts along heel, 9sts from needle, 6sts along heel, k16 from instep sts, move round marker to here and last stitch to left hand needle. Cont as folls:

ROUND 1: s1, k1, psso, 5M, 2C, 6M, 2C, 3M, 2togM, 5M, 2C, 6M, 2C, 1M.

ROUND 2: s1, k1, psso, 3M, 4C, 4M, 4C, 1M, 2togM, *4M, 4C* twice.

ROUND 3: s1, k1, psso, 2M, 4C, 4M, 4C, 2togM, *4M, 4C* twice.

ROUND 4: *4M, 2C, 2M* to end.

Cont in patt to completion of round 24. Break C.

Shape toe
Using M,

ROUND 1: knit.

ROUND 2: *k2tog, k11, s1, k1, psso* twice.

ROUND 3: knit.

ROUND 4: *k2tog, k9, s1, k1, psso* twice.

ROUND 5: knit.

ROUND 6: *k2tog, k7, s1, k1, psso* twice.

ROUND 7: knit.

ROUND 8: bind (cast) off.

Second sock
Make second sock to match.

FINISHING
Join toe seam (see page 123).
Weave in any loose ends.

daisy lace bootees

The lace flower on the toes is pretty, but not too fussy, making these a great every-day bootee.

SIZE
To fit baby of 0–3 months

MATERIALS
Jaeger merino 4 ply
1¾oz (50g) ball each of
    cream (M)   1
    pink (C)   1
1 pair of US 2 (3mm) needles
39in (100cm) of ribbon

BEFORE YOU START
Gauge (Tension)
28sts and 38 rows = 4in (10cm) square over stockinette (stocking) stitch using US 2 (3mm) needles.

Abbreviations
See page 126.

BASIC KNIT
Cuff
Using C, cast on 41sts and work 10 rows in stockinette (stocking) stitch.
Change to M and work 6 rows.
ROW 7: k2, *yo, k2tog, k2* nine times, yo, k2tog, k1.
Work 3 more rows.

Divide for top of foot
K28, turn, p15 turn.
On 15sts, work 6 rows.
ROW 7: k7, yo, s1, k1, psso, k6.
ROW 8 AND ALT ROWS: purl.
ROW 9: k4, k2tog, yo, k3, yo, s1, k1, psso, k4.
ROW 11: k3, k2tog, yo, k2, yo, s1, k1, psso, k1, yo, s1, k1, psso, k3.
ROW 13: as row 9.
ROW 15: as row 7.
Work 7 more rows. Break yarn.
With RS facing, (13sts on needle), rejoin M and pick up 11sts along side of foot, 15sts from toe, 11sts along side of foot and 13sts on needle. (63sts)
Knit 13 rows.

Shape sole
ROW 1: k1, *k2tog, k25, k2tog* k3, *to* again, k1.
ROW 2: k26, k2tog, k3, k2tog, k26.
ROW 3: k1, *k2tog, k22, k2tog* k3, *to* again, k1.
ROW 4: k23, k2tog, k3, k2tog, k23.
ROW 5: k1, *k2tog, k19, k2tog* k3, *to* again, k1.
ROW 6: bind (cast) off.

Second bootee
Make second bootee to match.

FINISHING
Join leg seam and under foot seam. Weave in any loose ends. Cut ribbon in half, thread through eyelets and tie in bow (see page 123).

pixie boots

Perfect for your own little pixie, these lace-up boots are smart and original. You could knit them in a pale color and lace them with ribbons to make a little girl's feet especially pretty.

SIZE
To fit baby of 3–6 months

MATERIALS
Jaeger merino dk
1¾oz (50g) ball of
   green   1
Small amount of red
1 pair of US 3 (3¼mm) needles
Safety pin

BEFORE YOU START
Gauge (Tension)
24sts and 32 rows = 4in (10cm) square over stockinette (stocking) stitch using US 3 (3¼mm) needles.

Abbreviations
See page 126.

BASIC KNIT
Sole
Start at toe end. Cast on 2sts. Work in seed (moss) stitch. Inc each end rows 1, 3 and 5. Cont until work measures 2¾in (7cm). Dec each end next and alt rows to 2sts, k2tog, fasten off.

Upper
Start at toe end. Cast on 2sts.
ROW 1: inc in both sts.
ROW 2: k1, inc, inc, k1.
ROW 3: purl.
ROW 4: k1, inc in next 4sts, k1.
ROW 5: purl.
ROW 6: k3, inc in next 4sts, k3.
ROW 7: purl.
ROW 8: k5, inc in next 4sts, k5. (18sts)
ROW 9: p4, seed (moss) 10, p4.
ROW 10: k4, seed (moss) 10, k4.
ROW 11: as row 9.
ROW 12: k4, seed (moss) 3, bind (cast) off 4sts, seed (moss) 3, k4.
ROW 13: p4, seed (moss) 3.
ROW 14: seed (moss) 3, k4.
ROW 15: p4, k1, yo, k2tog.
ROW 16: as row 14.
ROWS 17–22: as rows 13–14 three times.
ROWS 23–24: as rows 15–16.
Row 25: purl 4, place 3sts on safety pin.
Work 10 rows in stockinette (stocking) stitch.
Bind (cast) off.
Rejoin yarn to remaining sts and work to match.
Join heel seam.

Cuff
With RS facing, seed (moss) 3 from safety pin, pick up and knit 9sts to heel, 1st from seam, 9sts from heel to safety pin, seed (moss) 3.
ROWS 1–4: seed (moss) 3, rib 19, seed (moss) 3
ROW 5: k2tog, yo, seed (moss) 1, rib 19, seed (moss) 1, yo, k2tog.
ROWS 6–10: as row 1 five times.
ROW 11: as row 5.
ROWS 12–13: bind (cast) off 3, work to end.
ROW 14: seed (moss) 3, purl to last 3sts, seed (moss) 3.
ROW 15: seed (moss) 3, m1, knit to last 3sts, m1, seed (moss) 3.
ROW 16: as row 14.
ROW 17: seed (moss) 3, knit to last 3sts, seed (moss) 3.
ROW 18: seed (moss) 3, m1, purl to last 3sts, m1, seed (moss) 3.
ROWS 19–20: as rows 15–16.
ROWS 21–23: seed (moss).
ROW 24: bind (cast) off.

Second boot
Make second boot to match.

FINISHING
Weave in any loose ends. Plait three lengths of red yarn together to make laces, knotting ends to secure them. Thread laces through eyelets (see photograph and page 123).

gingham shoes

A design for more experienced fair isle knitters, these shoes are so pretty and sweet that, tied with a sheer ribbon, they are perfect for little princesses.

SIZE
To fit baby of 6–9 months

MATERIALS
Rowan cotton glacé
1¾oz (50g) balls each of
pink (M)   1
white (C)   1
1 pair US 2 (2¾mm) needles
16in (40cm) of ribbon

BEFORE YOU START
Gauge (Tension)
26sts and 34 rows = 4in (10cm) square over Fair Isle using US 2 (2¾mm) needles.

Abbreviations
See page 126.

BASIC KNIT
Sole
Using M, cast on 24sts and work in seed (moss) stitch.
Inc each end of rows 2, 4, 6, and 8. *(32sts)*
Work 3 rows. Dec each end of rows 12, 14, 16 and 18. *(24sts)*
Row 19: seed (moss) to end, cast on 8sts.

Upper
Change to stocking (stockinette) stitch.
ROW 1: *3M, 3C* to last 2sts, 2M.
ROW 2: inc, 1M, *3C, 3M* to end.
ROW 3: *3M, 3C* to last 3sts, 3M.
ROW 4: inc, 2M, *3C, 3M* to end.
ROW 5: *3C, 3M* to last 4sts, 3C, 1M.
ROW 6: inc, *3C, 3M* to last 3sts, 3C.
ROW 7: *3C, 3M* to last 5sts, 3C, 2M.
ROW 8: inc, 1M, *3C, 3M* to last 3sts, 3C.
ROW 9: *3M, 3C* to end.
ROW 10: inc, 2C, *3M, 3C* twice, 21M.
ROW 11: using M, *k1, p1* six times, yo, p2tog, *k1, p1* three times, knit *3C, 3M* twice, 3C, 1M.
ROW 12: inc, purl *3C, 3M* twice, 3C, using M, *k1, p1* to last st, k1.
ROW 13: using M, bind (cast) off 18sts, k1, p1, k1, knit *3M, 3C* twice, 3M, 2C.
ROW 14: purl 2C, *3M, 3C* twice, using M, p3, k1, p1, k1.
ROW 15: using M, k1, p1, k4, knit *3C, 3M* twice, 2C.
ROWS 16–24: keep gingham patt correct (3sts/4rows), with 3 stitch seed (moss) edging in M.
ROW 25: cast on 18sts, using M, *k1, p1* six times, yo, p2tog, *k1, p1* three times, k1, knit *3C, 3M* twice, 3M, 2C.
ROW 26: p2togM, *3C, 3M* twice, 3C, seed (moss) 21sts.

ROW 27: using M, seed (moss) 21, knit *3C, 3M* twice, 3C, 1M.
ROW 28: p2togC, purl 2C *3M, 3C* to end.
ROWS 29–36: Work 8 rows in gingham patt, dec beg of each purl row.
ROW 37: bind (cast) off.

Edging
With RS facing and using M, pick up 21sts from heel to front, 12sts across gingham and 21sts from front to heel. Work as folls:–
ROW 1: seed (moss) 12, dec, yo, seed (moss) 6, dec, seed (moss) 10, dec, seed (moss) 6, yo, dec, seed (moss) 12.
ROWS 2: seed (moss) stitch.
ROW 3: bind (cast) off.

Second shoe
Make second shoe to match.

FINISHING
Join heel seam. Carefully fit upper to sole, easing fullness around toe area, and stitch into position. Weave in any loose ends. Cut ribbon in half, thread through eyelets and tie in bow (see page 123).

lace and heart bootees
A combination of lacey cuffs and an intarsia motif make these charming bootees a good design for more experienced knitters to try their hand at. Ribbon ties will help to keep the bootees securely on a baby's feet.

SIZE
To fit baby of 3–6(6–9) months

MATERIALS
Rowan true 4 ply botany
1¾oz (50g) ball of
    cream (M)   1
Small amount of red (C)
1 pair each of US 3 (3¼mm) and
US 2 (3mm) needles
39in (100cm) of ribbon

BEFORE YOU START
Gauge (Tension)
28sts and 38 rows = 4in
(10cm) square over stockinette
(stocking) stitch using US 3
(3¼mm) needles.

Abbreviations
See page 126.

BASIC KNIT
Cuff
Using C and US 3 (3¼mm)
needles, cast on 51sts.
Change to M.
ROW 1: knit.
ROW 2: k2, yo, k2, s1, k2tog, psso,
k2, *yo, k1, yo, k2, s1, k2tog,
psso, k2* five times, yo, k2.
ROWS 3–18: as rows 1–2
eight times.
ROW 19: knit.
ROW 20: change to US 2 (3mm)
needles, p2, *p2tog, p3* nine
times, p2tog, p2. *(41sts)*
Change to stocking (stockinette)
stitch. Work 2 rows.
ROW 3: k2, *yo, k2tog, k2* nine
times, yo, k2tog, k1.
Work 3 more rows.

Divide for top of foot
K28, turn, p15, turn.
On 15sts, work 6(8) rows.

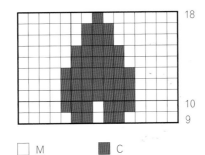

ROW 7(9): place heart motif
following instructions and chart:
knit 5M, 2C, 1M, 2C, 5M,
Work heart motif then work 2(4)
more rows (toe), break yarn.
With RS facing, *(13sts on needle)*,
rejoin M and pick up 11(16)sts
along side of foot, 15sts from toe,
11(16)sts along side of foot and
13sts on needle. *(63:73sts)*
Knit 13 rows.

Shape sole
ROW 1: k1, *k2tog, k25(30),
k2tog* k3, *to* again, k1.
ROW 2: k26(31), k2tog, k3,
k2tog, k26(31).
ROW 3: k1, *k2tog, k22(27),
k2tog* k3, *to* again, k1.
ROW 4: k23(28), k2tog, k3,
k2tog, k23(28).
ROW 5: k1, *k2tog, k19(24),
k2tog* k3, *to* again, k1.
ROW 6: bind (cast) off.

Second bootee
Make second bootee to match.

FINISHING
Join leg seam and under foot
seam. Weave in any loose
ends. Cut ribbon in half, thread
through eyelets and tie in bow
(see page 123).

pirate boots

This stripy design is perfect for bold little boys and as the boots are knitted in wool, they will keep little feet warm on the windiest days out.

SIZE
To fit baby of 3–6 months

MATERIALS
Jaeger merino dk
1¾oz (50g) ball each of
blue (A)   1
cream (B)   1
red (C)   1
1 pair of US 2 (2¾mm) needles

BEFORE YOU START
Gauge (Tension)
24sts and 32 rows = 4in (10cm) square over stockinette (stocking) stitch using US 2 (2¾mm) needles.

Abbreviations
See page 126.

BASIC KNIT
Sole
Start at heel end. Using C, cast on 3sts and work in seed (moss) stitch. Inc each end of rows 2, 3, 5, 6 and 8. (13sts).
Cont without shaping to completion of row 36. Dec each end of next and every alt row to 5sts.
NEXT ROW: purl.
Change to stockinette (stocking) stitch and work in stripes of 4 rows B, 4 rows A. Shaping rows only given.

Upper
ROW 1: inc in 4sts, k1. (9sts)
ROW 3: k1, inc in 2sts, k2, inc in 2sts, k2. (13sts)
ROW 5: k2, inc in 2sts, k4, inc in 2sts, k3. (17sts)
ROW 7: k3, inc, k8, inc, k4. (19sts)
ROW 10: *p2, inc* twice, p6, *inc, p2* twice, p1. (23sts)
ROW 25: k10, bind (cast) off 3sts, k10.
On 10sts
ROW 27: k1, k2tog, knit to end.
ROW 29: as row 27.
ROW 31: as row 27. (7sts)
Work to completion of row 46. Bind (cast) off.
Rejoin yarn to remaining sts at center front.
ROW 26: WS facing, purl.
ROW 27: knit to last 3sts, s1, k1, psso, k1.
Cont decs as set and work to match first side.

Cuff
With RS facing and using C, pick up and knit 35sts around ankle. Work 11 rows in k1, p1 rib. Bind (cast) off.

Second boot
Make second boot to match.

FINISHING
Join cuff and heel seam, pin to heel end of sole. Carefully pin upper to sole, easing any excess around toe area, and stitch into position (see page 123). Weave in any loose ends.

sheep bootees

Soft and fluffy, these bootees will look lovely on your own little lamb.
Ribbons in the cuffs will help to keep them in place.

sheep bootees cont

SIZE
To fit baby aged 3–6 months

MATERIALS
Jaeger merino dk
1¾oz (50g) ball of
    black (B)   1
Jaeger persia
1¾oz (50g) ball of
    cream (C)   1
1 pair each of US 3 (3¼mm) and
US 7 (4½mm) needles
30in (76cm) of ribbon

BEFORE YOU START
Gauge (Tension)
16sts and 26 rows = 4in (10cm)
square over stockinette (stocking)
stitch using Jaeger Persia and
US 7 (4½mm) needles.

Abbreviations
See page 126.

BASIC KNIT
Sole
Using US 3 (3¼mm) needles
and B, cast on 3sts. Work in
garter stitch.
Inc each end of first and every alt
row to 9sts.
Cont without shaping until work
measures 3½in (9cm).
Dec each end of next and every
alt row to 3sts. Bind (cast) off.

Back and heel
Using US 7 (4½mm) needles and
C, cast on 18sts and work 6 rows
in stockinette (stocking) stitch.
ROWS 7–10: work in k1, p1 rib.
Work 10 more rows in stockinette
(stocking) stitch, inc each end of
rows 1, 3 and 5. Bind (cast) off.

Front and toe
Using US 7 (4½mm) needles and
C, cast on 8sts.
ROW 1: k2, inc in next 3sts, k3.
ROW 2: purl.
ROW 3: k2, inc in next 6sts, k3.
(17sts)
ROW 4: purl.
Work 15 rows more in stockinette
(stocking) stitch.
ROW 20: bind (cast) off knitwise.
Mark 7th and 10th sts (C1 and C2
in fig 2 on page 127).

Ears (make 2)
Using US 3 (3¼mm) needles and
B, cast on 8sts and work 5 rows
in stockinette (stocking) stitch.
Dec each end of next 2 rows.
Work 1 row.
Inc each end of next 2 rows.
Work 4 more rows. Bind (cast) off.

Second bootee
Make second bootee to match.

FINISHING
Refer to figs 1 and 2 on page 127.
Front and toe – purl side is right
side. Fold front in half lengthwise
and join cast on edge, A to A, to
make toe, see fig 2.
Back and heel – knit side is right
side. Join back and heel section
to front by stitching seams B1-C1
and B2-C2, see figs 1 and 2.
Join upper to sole. Weave in any
loose ends.
Fold ears in half and stitch side
seams, then stitch to bootees.
Embroider nose and eyes using
black yarn (see photograph). Turn
over cuff at ankle and stitch down.
Cut ribbon in half and thread
through cuff (see page 123).

herringbone bootees
With their understated textured cuffs and scalloped trim, these bootees are ideal for special occasions as well as every-day wear.

SIZE
To fit baby of 0–3(3–6) months

MATERIALS
Rowan 4 ply cotton
1¾oz (50g) ball of
    pale blue (M)   1
Small amount of white (C)
1 pair of US 2 (3mm) needles

BEFORE YOU START
Gauge (Tension)
28sts and 38 rows = 4in (10cm) square over stockinette (stocking) stitch using US 2 (3mm) needles.

Abbreviations
m1 = place yarn before next stitch onto left hand needle and knit it.
See also page 126.

BASIC KNIT
Cuff
Using C, cast on 51sts. Change to M and work as folls:
ROW 1: (WS) purl.
ROW 2: k1, k2tog, *k2, m1, k1, m1, k2, s1, k2tog, psso* five times, k2, m1, k1, m1, k2, s1, k1, psso, k1.
Repeat rows 1 and 2 until work measures 1½in (4cm), ending with row 2.
NEXT ROW: *p2, p2tog, p1* to last st, p1. *(41sts)*
Work 1¼in (3cm) in k1, p1 rib, ending with a RS row.
WS facing, change to stockinette (stocking) stitch, (first row, knit) and work 4 rows.

Divide for top of foot
K28 turn, p15 turn.
On 15sts, work 16(22) rows.
Break yarn.
With RS facing, *(13sts on needle)*, rejoin M and pick up 11(17)sts along side of foot, 15sts from toe, 11(17)sts along side of foot and 13sts on needle. *(63:75sts)*
Knit 13 rows.

Shape sole
ROW 1: k1, *k2tog, k25(31), k2tog* k3, *to* again, k1.
ROW 2: k26(32), k2tog, k3, k2tog, k26(32).
ROW 3: k1, *k2tog, k22(28), k2tog* k3, *to* again, k1.
ROW 4: k23(29), k2tog, k3, k2tog, k23(29).
ROW 5: k1, *k2tog, k19(25), k2tog* k3, *to* again, k1.
ROW 6: bind (cast) off.

Second bootee
Make second bootee to match.

FINISHING
Join leg seam and under foot seam (see page 123). Weave in any loose ends.

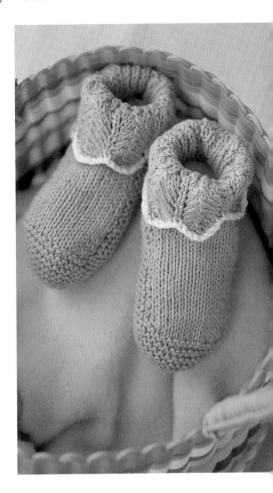

fleur de lys socks

This is a traditional and slightly more complicated design that is perfect for more experienced knitters who enjoy working fair isle patterns.

SIZE
To fit baby of 3–6 months

MATERIALS
Jaeger merino 4 ply
1¾oz (50g) ball of
   cream (M)   1
Small amounts of red (A)
   and blue (B)
4 double-ended US 2
(3mm) needles

BEFORE YOU START
Gauge (Tension)
28sts and 38 rows = 4in (10cm) square over stockinette (stocking) stitch using US 2 (3mm) needles.

Abbreviations
See page 126.

BASIC KNIT
Note: place marker at beginning of round.

Cuff
Using B, cast on 32sts (10, 10 and 12sts). Work 5 rounds in ∗k1, p1∗ to end.
ROUND 6: knit ∗3M, 1A∗ to end.
ROUND 7: ∗1A, 1M, 2A∗ to end.
ROUND 8: as round 6.
ROUND 9: ∗1M, 1B, 2M∗ to end.
ROUND 10: ∗3B, 1M∗ to end.
ROUND 11: as round 9.
ROUNDS 12–17: as rounds 6–11.
ROUNDS 18–20: as rounds 6–8.

Start heel
ROUND 21: using B, k15, turn, leave remaining sts on needles for instep.
On 15sts, work 7 rows in stockinette (stocking) stitch, starting with a purl row.

Shape heel
ROW 1: k9, turn.
ROW 2: s1, p2 turn.
ROW 3: s1, k1, s1, k1, psso, k1, turn.
ROW 4: s1, p2, p2tog, p1, turn.
ROW 5: s1, k3, s1, k1, psso, k1, turn.
ROW 6: s1, p4, p2tog, p1, turn.
ROW 7: s1, k5, s1, k1, psso, turn.
ROW 8: s1, p6, p2tog, p1.
Break yarn.
Using B, pick up and knit 6sts from side heel, knit 9sts from needle, pick up and knit 6sts from side of heel. Break yarn.

RIGHT SIDE FACING: **return to round marker.** Take last stitch of last round and move it to left hand needle to be first stitch of round. Cont as folls:
ROUND 1: s1, 1B, psso, ∗3M, 1B∗ four times, 3M, 2togB, 1M, ∗1B, 3M∗ three times, 1B, 1M.
ROUND 2: s1, 1B, psso, ∗1M, 3B∗ four times, 1M, 2togM, ∗3B, 1M∗ three times, 3B.
ROUND 3: s1, 1M, psso, 1M, ∗1B, 3M∗ three times, 1B, 1M, 2togM, 1M, ∗1B, 3M∗ three times, 1B, 1M.
ROUNDS 4–24: continue in patt. Break M and A.

Shape toe
Using B,
ROUND 1: knit.
ROUND 2: ∗k2tog, k12, s1, k1, psso∗ twice.
ROUND 3: knit.
ROUND 4: ∗k2tog, k10, s1, k1, psso∗ twice.
ROUND 5: knit.
ROUND 6: ∗k2tog, k8, s1, k1, psso∗ twice.
ROUND 7: knit.
ROUND 8: bind (cast) off.

Second sock
Make second sock to match.

FINISHING
Join toe seam (see page 123).
Weave in any loose ends.

knot shoes
These lovely, fluffy shoes simply tie round a baby's foot for a perfect fit, and look very modern and stylish, too.

SIZE
To fit baby of 0–3 months

MATERIALS
Rowan kidsilk haze
1oz (25g) ball of
    orange   1
1 pair of US 2 (2¾mm) needles

BEFORE YOU START
Gauge (Tension)
28sts and 28 rows = 4in (10cm) square over garter stitch using US 2 (2¾mm) needles.

Abbreviations
See page 126.

BASIC KNIT
Note: use two ends of yarn throughout.

Sole
Cast on 24sts and work in garter stitch.
Inc each end of rows 2, 4, 6, and 8. *(32sts)*
Work 3 rows. Dec each end of rows 12, 14, 16 and 18. *(24sts)*
ROW 19: knit to end, cast on 8sts.

Upper
ROW 1: knit.
ROW 2: inc, knit to end.
ROWS 3–12: as rows 1–2 five times. *(38sts)*
ROW 13: bind (cast) off 19sts, knit to end.
ROWS 14–25: knit.
ROW 26: knit to end, cast on 19sts.
ROW 27: knit.
ROW 28: k2tog, knit to end.
ROWS 29–38: as 27–28 five times.
ROW 39: bind (cast) off.

Ties (make 2)
Using US 2 (2¾mm) needles, cast on 40sts.
ROW 1: knit.
ROW 2: bind (cast) off 2sts, knit to end.
ROW 3: knit to last 2sts, k2tog.
ROWS 4–5: as rows 2–3.
ROW 6: bind (cast) off.

Second shoe
Make second shoe to match.

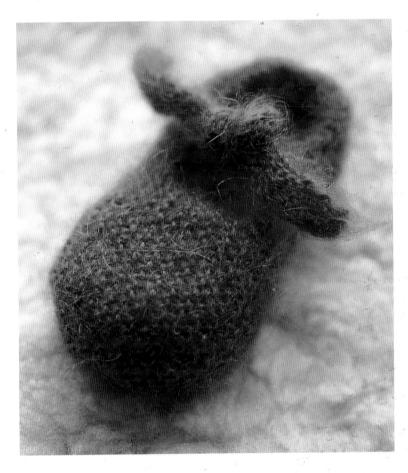

FINISHING
Join heel seam. Carefully fit upper to sole, easing fullness around toe area, and stitch into position. Weave in any loose ends. Sew the square end of tie to each side of shoe, approx ½in (1cm) from front (see photograph and page 123).

zebra bootees

Fashionable and funky for trendy toes, these bootees are practical, too, as the deep cuffs will help to keep them firmly on wriggling feet and kicking legs.

SIZE
To fit baby of 3–6 months

MATERIALS
Rowan cotton glacé
1¾oz (50g) balls each of
    black (A)   1
    cream (B)   1
1 pair of US 2 (2¾mm) needles.

BEFORE YOU START
Gauge (Tension)
26sts and 34 rows = 4in (10cm)
square over stockinette (stocking)
stitch using US 2 (2¾mm) needles.

Abbreviations
See page 126.

BASIC KNIT
Sole
Start at heel end. Using A, cast on
3sts and work in seed (moss)
stitch. Inc each end of rows 2, 3,
5, 6 and 8. *(13sts)*
Cont without shaping to
completion of row 36.
Dec each end of next and every
alt row to 5sts.
NEXT ROW: purl.

Upper
Cont in stocking
(stockinette) stitch.
ROW 1: inc A, inc B, 1A, inc B,
inc A. *(9sts)*
ROW 2: 2A, 2B, 1A, 2B, 2A.

ROW 3: 1A, inc A, inc B, 1B, 1A, 1B,
inc B, inc A, 1A. *(13sts)*
ROW 4: 3A, 2B, 2A, 3B, 3A.
ROW 5: 2A, inc A, inc B, 1B, 3A,
1B, inc B, inc A, 2A. *(17sts)*
ROW 6: 3A, 3B, 2A, 1B, 2A, 3B, 3A.
ROW 7: 3A, inc B, *1B, 1A* twice,
inc B, 1B, 3A. *(19sts)*
ROW 8: 2A, 3B, 4A, 2B, 3A, 3B, 2A.
ROW 9: 1A, 3B, 4A, 2B, 4A, 3B, 2A.
ROW 10: 2A, inc A, 2B, inc A, 1B,
2A, 2B, 1A, 1B, inc A, 2A, inc B,
2B. *(23sts)*
ROWS 11–44: work zebra pattern
following chart.
ROW 45: bind (cast) off.
Rejoin yarn to rem sts center front.
ROW 26: WS facing, 1B, 3A, 1B, 2A.
ROW 27: 1B, 3A, 1B, 2A, s1, 1B,
psso, 1B.
Cont decs as set and work to
match first side.

Cuff
With RS facing and using A, pick
up 35sts around ankle.
Work 26 rows in k1, p1 rib.
WS facing, change to B and knit
1 row. Bind (cast) off.

Second bootee
Make second bootee to match.

FINISHING
Join cuff seam, pin to heel end of
sole. Carefully pin upper to sole,
easing any excess around toe
area, and stitch into position (see
page 123). Weave in loose ends.

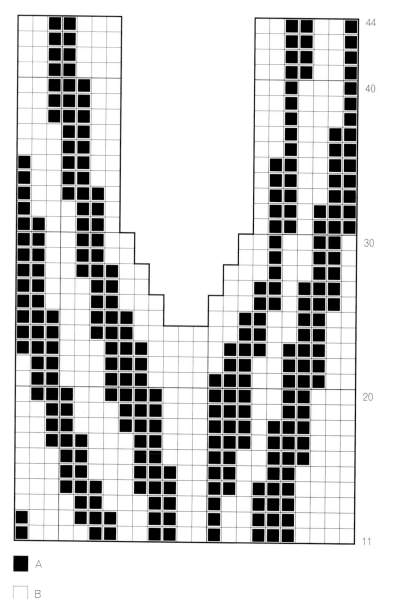

■ A
□ B

heart t-bar shoes
The classic t-bar shoe is given extra appeal with a simple heart motif. Try knitting the shoes in a pastel color with a pale heart as well.

SIZE
To fit baby of 3–6 months

MATERIALS
Rowan cotton glacé
1¾oz (50g) ball of
    dark blue (M)   1
Small amount of red (C)
1 pair of US 3 (3¼mm) needles
2 small buttons

BEFORE YOU START
Gauge (Tension)
26sts and 30 rows = 4in (10cm) square over Fair Isle using US 3 (3¼mm) needles.

Abbreviations
See page 126.

BASIC KNIT
Sole
Using M, cast on 19sts and work in seed (moss) stitch.
Inc each end of rows 2, 4 and 6. *(25sts)*
Work 2 rows. Dec each end of rows 9, 11 and 13. *(19sts)*
ROW 14: bind (cast) off.

Upper
Using M, cast on 59sts. Work as folls:
ROWS 1–9: *k1, p1* to last st, k1.
ROW 10: RS facing, seed (moss) 24, k10, s1, k1, psso, turn.
ROW 11: s1, p9, p2tog, turn.
ROW 12: place heart motif following instructions and chart: s1, knit 4M, 1C, 4M, s1, k1, psso, turn.
ROW 13: s1, purl 3M, 3C, 3M, p2tog, turn.
ROW 14: s1, knit 2M, 5C, 2M, s1, k1, psso, turn.
ROW 15: s1, purl 2M, 5C, 2M, p2tog, turn.
ROW 16: s1, knit 1M, 7C, 1M, s1, k1, psso, turn.
ROW 17: s1, purl 1M, 7C, 1M, p2tog, turn.
ROW 18: s1, knit 2M, 2C, 1M, 2C, 2M, s1, k1, psso, turn. Break C.
ROW 19: as row 11.
ROW 20: s1, k9, s1, k1, psso, turn.
ROW 21: as row 11. *(47sts)*
ROW 22: s1, *p1, k1* to end.
ROW 23: seed (moss) across all sts, marking sts 8 and 39.

ROW 24: **bind (cast) off 22sts, seed (moss) 3sts, bind (cast) off 22sts.**

Strap A
Rejoin yarn to 3sts and work 2½in (6cm) in seed (moss) stitch. Bind (cast) off.

Second shoe
Make second shoe to match.

FINISHING
Weave in any loose ends.

Right strap B
Join heel seam. Cast on 3sts, with RS facing pick up and knit 17sts around heel between marked stitches, cast on 15sts, work
as folls:
ROW 1: *k1, p1* to last st, k1.
ROW 2: *k1, p1* to last 4sts, p2tog, yo, p1, k1.
ROW 3: as row 1.
ROW 4: bind (cast) off.

Left strap B
Cast on 15sts, with RS facing, pick up and knit 17sts around heel between marked sts, cast on 3sts, work as folls:
ROW 1: *k1, p1* to last st, k1.
ROW 2: k1, p1, yo, p2tog, *k1, p1* to last st, k1.
ROW 3: as row 1.
ROW 4: bind (cast) off.

Carefully pin sole to upper and stitch into position. Weave in any loose ends. Fold center strap (A) over to make loop for cross strap. Stitch in place. Thread strap (B) through loop. Sew on buttons (see page 123).

bee shoes

These fun little shoes are bold and simple and are bound to get you, and your baby, noticed.

bee shoes cont

SIZE
To fit baby of 3–6 months

MATERIALS
Rowan cotton glacé
1¾oz (50g) ball each of
black (A)	1
yellow (B)	1
1 pair of US 2 (2¾mm) needles

BEFORE YOU START
Gauge (Tension)
26sts and 34 rows = 4in (10cm) square over stockinette (stocking) stitch using US 2 (2¾mm) needles.

Abbreviations
See page 126.

BASIC KNIT
Sole
Start at heel end. Using A, cast on 3sts and work in seed (moss) stitch. Inc each end of rows 2, 3, 5, 6 and 8. *(13sts)*
Cont without shaping to completion of row 36. Dec each end of next and every alt row to 5sts.
NEXT ROW: purl.
Change to stockinette (stocking) stitch and work in stripes of 4 rows B, 4 rows A. Shaping rows only given.

Upper
ROW 1: inc in 4sts, k1. *(9sts)*
ROW 3: k1, inc in 2sts, k2, inc in 2sts, k2. *(13sts)*
ROW 5: k2, inc in 2sts, k4, inc in 2sts, k3. *(17sts)*
ROW 7: k3, inc, k8, inc, k4. *(19sts)*
ROW 10: *p2, inc* twice, p6, *inc, p2* twice, p1. *(23sts)*
ROW 25: k10, bind (cast) off 3sts, k10.
On 10sts
ROW 27: k1, k2tog, knit to end.
ROW 29: as row 27.
ROW 31: as row 27. *(7sts)*
Work to completion of row 46.
Bind (cast) off.
Rejoin yarn to remaining sts at center front.
ROW 26: WS facing, purl.
ROW 27: knit to last 3sts, s1, k1, psso, k1.
Cont decs as set and work to match first side.

Trim
Using A, pick up 3sts in every 4 rows around ankle.
Bind (cast) off.

Second shoe
Make second shoe to match.

FINISHING
Join heel seam, pin to heel end of sole. Carefully pin upper to sole, easing any excess around toe area, and stitch into position (see page 123). Weave in any loose ends.

simple slippers
These are perfect for a novice knitter. They are quick and simple to knit and can be embellished with a felt motif, tiny buttons or beads, or just left plain.

SIZE
To fit baby of 0–3 months

MATERIALS
Choose from
❶ Star simple slippers
Rowan wool cotton
1¾oz (50g) ball of
    blue   1
Yellow felt

❷ Flower simple slippers
Rowan wool cotton
1¾oz (50g) ball of
    red   1
White felt
2 buttons

1 pair of US 6 (4mm) needles

BEFORE YOU START
Gauge (Tension)
22sts and 40 rows = 4in (10cm)
square over garter stitch using
US 6 (4mm) needles.

Abbreviations
See page 126.

BASIC KNIT
Sole
Cast on 14sts. Working in garter
stitch (every row knit), inc each
end of rows 1, 3, 5 and 7. Dec
each end of rows 9, 11, 13 and 15.
(14sts)

Upper
ROW 16: cast on 5sts (for heel), k19.
Inc beg rows (toe) 17, 19, 21
and 23.
ROW 24: bind (cast) off 10sts, purl
to end.
ROW 25: knit.
ROW 26: k2, purl to end.
ROWS 27–30: as rows 25–26 twice.
ROW 31: knit.
ROW 32: cast on 10sts, k23.
Dec beg rows 33, 35, 37 and 39.
(19sts)
Bind (cast) off.

Second slipper
Make second slipper to match.

FINISHING
Join heel seam. Pin upper
around sole, easing excess
material around toe, and stitch
into position (see page 123).
Weave in any loose ends.

❶ Star simple slipper
Trace star motif, cut out of yellow
felt and stitch to toe of slipper
(see photograph and page 123).

❷ Flower simple slipper
Trace daisy motif, cut out of white
felt and stitch to toe of slipper,
using button to hold in place (see
photograph and page 123).

animal bootees

For bouncing bunnies and baby bears everywhere, these bootees are perfect. Ribbed cuffs and shaped uppers will help to keep them on busy feet.

SIZE
To fit a baby of 6–9 months

MATERIALS
Choose from
❶ Bunny bootee
Jaeger merino dk
1¾oz (50g) ball each of

beige (A)	1
cream (B)	1
pink (C)	1

Small amount of brown

❷ Bear bootee
Jaeger merino dk
1¾oz (50g) ball each of

cream (A)	1
camel (B)	1
brown (C)	1

1 pair of US 2 (3mm) needles

BEFORE YOU START
Gauge (Tension)
26sts and 36 rows = 4in (10cm) square over stockinette (stocking) stitch using US 2 (3mm) needles.

Abbreviations
See page 126.

BASIC KNIT
Sole
Using A, cast on 53sts.
ROW 1: *inc, k24, inc* twice, k1.
ROWS 2–4: knit.
ROW 5: *inc, k26, inc* twice, k1.
ROWS 6–8: knit.
ROW 9: *inc, k28, inc* twice, k1.
ROW 10: knit.

Edging
Work picot edge.
Change to C.
ROW 1: knit.
ROW 2: purl.
ROW 3: k1, *yo, k2tog* to end.
ROW 4: purl.
ROWS 5–6: as rows 1–2.
Change to B.
ROW 7: fold work at row of holes and knit together, 1st from needle and 1st from FIRST row of picot, all across row.
ROWS 8–20: knit.

Divide for top of foot
ROW 1: k36, k2tog, turn.
ROW 2: k8, s1, k1, psso, turn.
ROW 3: k8, k2tog, turn.
ROWS 4–23: as rows 2–3 ten times. *(41sts)*
ROW 24: as row 2.
ROWS 25–28: knit across all sts.
Change to A and knit 1 row.

❶

Cuff
Change to k1, p1 rib and work 27 rows.
Change to C.
ROW 29: purl.
ROW 30: bind (cast) off knitwise.

Second bootee
Make second bootee to match.

SELECT ONE
❶ Bunny ears
Using B, cast on 8sts. Work 23 rows in stockinette (stocking) stitch, dec each end of rows 15, 19 and 23. Change to A and work 23 rows in stockinette (stocking) stitch (starting with a purl row), inc each end of rows 2, 4 and 8. Bind (cast) off.
Make three more ears to match.

❷

❷ Bear ears

Using B, cast on 8sts. Work
7 rows in stockinette (stocking)
stitch, dec each end of rows 6
and 7. Change to C and work
7 rows in stockinette (stocking)
stitch (starting with a purl row),
inc each end of rows 2 and 3.
Bind (cast) off.
Make three more ears to match.

FINISHING

Using a flat seam, join foot, heel
and back of ankle. Weave in any
loose ends. Join ear side seams.
Stitch base of ears to bootees
(see page 123). Embroider faces
using brown (see photograph).

stripy shoes
These shoes can be knitted in a wide range of colorways, and plaited ties will help to keep them firmly attached to a tot's tootsies.

SIZE
To fit baby of 3–6 months

MATERIALS
Rowan 4 ply cotton
1¾oz (50g) ball each of
    dark blue (M)   1
    light blue (C)   1
1 pair of US 2 (2¾mm) needles

BEFORE YOU START
Gauge (Tension)
28sts and 38 rows = 4in (10cm) square over stockinette (stocking) stitch using US 2 (2¾mm) needles.

Abbreviations
See page 126.

BASIC KNIT
Sole
Using M, cast on 24sts and work in seed (moss) stitch.
Inc each end of rows 2, 4, 6, and 8. (32sts)
Work 3 rows. Dec each end of rows 12, 14, 16 and 18. (24sts)
ROW 19: seed (moss) to end, cast on 8sts.

Upper
ROW 1: using C, knit.
ROW 2: inc, purl to end.
ROWS 3–4: using M, as rows 1–2.
ROW 5–8: as rows 1–4.
ROWS 9–10: as rows 1–2.
ROW 11: using C, bind (cast) off 21sts, using M, k16.
ROW 12: inc, p15.
ROW 13: using C, k17.
ROW 14: p17.
ROW 15–16: using M, as rows 13–14.
ROWS 17–24: as rows 13–16 three times.
ROW 25–26: as rows 13–14.
ROW 27: as row 15.
ROW 28: p2tog, p15, cast on 21sts
ROW 29: using C, knit.
ROW 30: p2tog, purl to end.
ROWS 31–38: work in stripy patt, dec beg of each purl row.
ROW 39: bind (cast) off.

Edging
With RS facing and using M, pick up 21sts from heel to front, 10sts across stripes and 21sts from front to heel.
ROW 1: seed (moss) 12, bind (cast) off 1, seed (moss) 7, dec, seed (moss) 8, dec, seed (moss) 7, bind (cast) off 1, seed (moss) 12.
ROW 2: seed (moss) 12, yo, seed (moss) 24, yo, seed (moss) 12.
ROW 3: bind (cast) off.

Make ties
Cut three 18in (46cm) lengths of M and thread halfway through an eyelet. With one end from each side of eyelet – two strands for each section – plait to end and knot. Trim ends.

Second shoe
Make second shoe to match.

FINISHING
Join heel seam. Carefully fit upper to sole, easing fullness around toe area, and stitch into position (see page 123. Weave in loose ends.

denim shoes

Yee-haa! Denim shoes for all little cowgirls. They will look better and better with every wash as the color fades and the stitch detail becomes clearer.

SIZE
To fit baby of 6–9 months

MATERIALS
Rowan denim
1¾oz (50g) ball of
   blue denim   1
1 pair of US 3 (3¼mm) needles
Safety pin
10 small buttons

BEFORE YOU START
Gauge (Tension)
22sts and 30 rows = 4in (10cm)
square over stockinette (stocking)
stitch using US 3 (3¼mm) needles
before washing.

Abbreviations
See page 126.

BASIC KNIT
Right shoe
Sole

Cast on 19sts and work in seed
(moss) stitch.
Inc each end of rows 2, 4, and 6.
(25sts)
Work 3 rows. Dec each end of
rows 10, 12 and 14. *(19sts)*
ROW 15: seed (moss) to end, cast
on 6sts.

Upper
ROW 1: knit.
ROW 2: inc, purl to end.
ROWS 3–6: as rows 1–2 twice.
ROW 7: knit.
ROW 8: inc, p10, seed (moss) 17.
ROW 9: seed (moss) 17, k12.
ROW 10: inc, p11, seed (moss) 17.
(30sts)
ROW 11: bind (cast) off 10sts, seed
(moss) 3, bind (cast) off 2sts,
seed (moss) 2, k13.
ROW 12: p13, seed (moss) 2, leave
3sts on safety pin.
ROW 13: seed (moss) 2, k13.
ROWS 14–21: as rows 12–13
four times.
ROW 22: p13, seed (moss) 2, cast
on 15sts.
ROW 23: seed (moss) 17, k13.
ROW 24: p2tog, p11, seed (moss) 17.
ROW 25: seed (moss) 17, k12.
ROW 26: p2tog, purl to end.
ROWS 27–32: work in stockinette
(stocking) stitch, dec beg of each
purl row. *(25sts)*
ROW 33: bind (cast) off.

Strap
Place 3sts from safety pin
onto needle.
ROWS 1–15: seed (moss) stitch.
ROW 16: seed (moss) 1, bind (cast)
off 1st, seed (moss) 1.
ROW 17: seed (moss) 1, yo, seed
(moss) 1.
ROWS 18–19: seed (moss) stitch.
ROW 20: bind (cast) off.

Left shoe
Sole
As for right shoe.

Upper
Reverse stockinette (stocking)
stitch, eg:
ROW 1: purl.
ROW 2: inc, knit to end.
ROW 8: inc, k10, seed (moss) 17.

FINISHING
Before sewing, machine wash
pieces plus length of yarn for
sewing at 60–70°C, spin and
tumble dry. Wash separately or
with other denim articles, as dye
comes out of yarn.
Join heel seam. Carefully fit upper
to sole, easing fullness around toe
area, and stitch into position.
Weave in any loose ends. Stitch
four decorative buttons to toe of
each shoe (see photograph) and
one button to fasten strap (see
page 123).

heel and toe socks

A classic sock design that looks fabulous in any colorway, these tiny socks are a perfect gift for any baby.

SIZE
To fit baby of 3–6 months

MATERIALS
Choose from
❶ Pink for a girl
Jaeger merino 4 ply
1¾oz (50g) balls each of
mid-pink (M)   1
dark pink (C)   1

❷ Blue for a boy
Jaeger merino 4 ply
1¾oz (50g) balls each of
mid-blue (M)   1
dark blue (C)   1

4 double-ended US 2
(3mm) needles

BEFORE YOU START
Gauge (Tension)
28sts and 38 rows = 4in (10cm) square over stockinette (stocking) stitch using US 2 (3mm) needles.

Abbreviations
See page 126.

BASIC KNIT
Note: place marker at beginning of round.

Cuff
Using M, cast on 32sts (10, 10 and 12sts). Work 5 rounds in *k1, p1* to end.
ROUNDS 7–20: *k3, p1* to end.
DO NOT BREAK M, join in C.

Start heel
ROUND 21: using C, k15, turn, leave remaining sts on needles for instep.
On 15sts, work 7 rows in stockinette (stocking) stitch, starting with a purl row.

Shape heel
ROW 1: k9, turn.
ROW 2: s1, p2, turn.
ROW 3: s1, k1, s1, k1, psso, k1, turn.
ROW 4: s1, p2, p2tog, p1, turn.
ROW 5: s1, k3, s1, k1, psso, k1, turn.
ROW 6: s1, p4, p2tog, p1, turn.
ROW 7: s1, k5, s1, k1, psso, turn.
ROW 8: s1, p6, p2tog, p1.
Break yarn.
Using M, pick up and knit 6sts along heel, 9sts from needle, 6sts along heel, *p1, k3* four times from instep, move round marker to here and last stitch to left hand needle.

Cont as folls:
ROUND 1: **p2tog, k19, p2tog,
k3, p1 three times, k3.**
ROUND 2: **p2tog, k17, p2tog,
k3, p1 three times, k3.**
ROUND 3: **p2tog, k15, p2tog,
k3, p1 three times, k3.**
ROUND 4: **p2tog, k13, p2tog,
k3, p1 three times, k3.**
ROUND 5: **p1, k13, *p1, k3*
four times.**
ROUNDS 6–24: **as round 5.**
Break M.

Shape toe
Using C,
ROUND 1: **knit.**
ROUND 2: ***k2tog, k11, s1, k1,
psso* twice.**
ROUND 3: **knit.**
ROUND 4: ***k2tog, k9, s1, k1,
psso* twice.**
ROUND 5: **knit.**
ROUND 6: ***k2tog, k7, s1, k1,
psso* twice.**
ROUND 7: **knit.**
ROUND 8: **bind (cast) off.**

Second sock
Make second sock to match.

FINISHING
Join toe seam (see page 123).
Weave in any loose ends.

textured-cuff bootees
The wool cotton mix is great for baby boots as the warmth of wool keeps feet snug and the crispness of cotton shows up textured stitches.

SIZE
To fit baby of 3–6 months

MATERIALS
Rowan wool cotton
1¾oz (50g) ball of
    cream   1
1 pair each of US 3 (3¼mm) and
US 6 (4mm) needles

BEFORE YOU START
Gauge (Tension)
22sts and 30 rows = 4in (10cm)
square over stockinette (stocking)
stitch using US 6 (4mm) needles.

Abbreviations
See page 126.

BASIC KNIT
Cuff
Using US 6 (4mm) needles, cast
on 27sts and work 10 rows in
seed (moss) stitch.
Change to US 3 (3¼mm) needles
and work 6 rows in k1, p1 rib.
Change to US 6 (4mm) needles
and stockinette (stocking) stitch
and work 4 rows.

Divide for top of foot
K18, turn, p9, turn.
On 9sts, work 12 rows stockinette
(stocking) stitch. Break yarn.
With RS facing, (9sts on needle),
pick up 10sts along side of foot,
9sts from toe, 10sts along side of
foot and 9sts on needle. *(47sts)*
Work 6 rows in stockinette
(stocking) stitch, starting with a
purl row.

Shape sole
ROW 7: knit.
ROW 8: k1, p2tog, *k1, p1* eight
times, k1, p2tog, k1, p1, k1, p2tog,
k1, p1 eight times, k1, p2tog, k1.
ROW 9: *k1, p1* to last st, k1.
ROW 10: k1, k2tog, seed (moss) 15,
p2tog, k1, p1, k1, p2tog, seed
(moss) 15, k2tog, k1.
ROW 11: k1, seed (moss) 16,
p1, k1 twice, p1, seed (moss)
16, k1.
ROW 12: k1, p2tog, seed (moss) 13,
p2tog, k1, p1, k1, p2tog, seed
(moss) 13, p2tog, k1.
ROW 13: as row 9.
ROW 14: bind (cast) off.

Second bootee
Make second bootee to match.

FINISHING
Join leg seam and under foot
seam (see page 123). Weave in
any loose ends.

bobble shoes

Colorful, fun and tactile, babies will love these jolly shoes. Be sure to sew the bobbles on securely so that little fingers can't cause trouble.

SIZE
To fit baby of 3–6 months

MATERIALS
Jaeger merino dk
1¾oz (50g) ball of
  navy   1
Small amounts of bright colors
  for bobbles
1 pair each of US 2 (3mm) and
US 6 (4mm) needles

BEFORE YOU START
Gauge (Tension)
26sts and 36 rows = 4in (10cm)
square over stockinette (stocking)
stitch using US 2 (3mm) needles.

Abbreviations
See page 126

BASIC KNIT
Sole
Start at heel end. Using US 2
(3mm) needles, cast on 3sts and
work in seed (moss) stitch. Inc
each end of rows 2, 3, 5, 6
and 8. *(13sts)*
Cont without shaping to
completion of row 36. Dec
each end of next and every alt
row to 5sts.
NEXT ROW: purl.
Change to stockinette (stocking)
stitch and work as folls (shaping
rows only given):

Upper
ROW 1: inc in 2sts, k1, inc in 2sts.
(9sts)
ROW 3: ✳k1, inc in next 2sts, k1✳
twice, k1. *(13sts)*
ROW 5: ✳k2, inc in next 2sts,
k2✳ twice, k1. *(17sts)*
ROW 7: k3, inc, k8, inc, k4. *(19sts)*
ROW 10: ✳p2, inc✳ twice, p6
✳inc, p2✳ twice, p1. *(23sts)*
ROW 25: k10, bind (cast) off
3sts, k10.
On 10sts
ROW 27: k1, k2tog, k7.
ROW 29: k1, k2tog, k6.
ROW 31: k1, k2tog, k5. *(7sts)*
ROW 45: bind (cast) off.
Rejoin yarn to remaining sts at
center front.
ROW 27: k7, s1, k1, psso, k1.
Cont decs as set and work to
match first side.

Edging

Using a bright color and US 2 (3mm) needles, pick up and knit 35sts around ankle.
Bind (cast) off.

Bobbles

Make as many different colored bobbles as you want for each shoe – we made eight for each one.
Using US 6 (4mm) and a bright color, cast on 3sts leaving a 4in (10cm) end for finishing.
ROW 1: inc, inc, k1.
ROW 2: purl.
ROW 3: knit.
ROW 4: purl.
ROW 5: s1, k1, psso, k1, k2tog.
ROW 6: p3tog.
ROW 7: fasten off, leaving a 4in (10cm) end for finishing.
Tie the two ends together tightly to make a bobble.

Second shoe

Make second shoe to match.

FINISHING

Join heel seam, pin to heel end of sole. Carefully pin upper to sole, easing any excess around toe area, and stitch into position. Weave in any loose ends. Using loose ends, stitch bobbles randomly to shoe (see page 123).

duck feet
Quack-quack, here comes a little duck.
These are here to make you laugh, though a firm cuff
makes them practical, too.

SIZE
To fit baby of 3–6 months

MATERIALS
Rowan cotton glacé
1¾oz (50g) ball of
   yellow   1
Small amount of orange
1 pair of US 3 (3¼mm) needles

BEFORE YOU START
Gauge (Tension)
24sts and 36 rows = 4in
(10cm) square over stockinette
(stocking) stitch using US 3
(3¼mm) needles.

Abbreviations
See page 126.

BASIC KNIT
Sole
Cast on 3sts. Working in seed
(moss) stitch, inc each end of
rows 2, 3, 5, and 7. (11sts)
Inc each end of rows 13, 19, 25,
31, 37 and 43. *(23sts)*
Work to completion of row 48.

Upper
Change to stockinette (stocking)
stitch and work 24 rows.
ROW 25: k10, bind (cast) off
3sts, k10.
On 10sts
ROW 26: purl.
ROW 27: k1, k2tog, knit to end.
ROWS 28–31: as rows 26–27 twice.
(7sts)
Work 13 more rows.
Bind (cast) off.
Rejoin yarn to remaining sts at
center edge.
ROW 26: purl.
ROW 27: knit to last 3sts, s1, k1,
psso, k1.
Work to match first side.

Cuff
With RS facing, pick up 36sts
around ankle. Work 26 rows in
k2, p2 rib. Bind (cast) off.

Second foot
Make second foot to match.

FINISHING
Join cuff and heel seam. Join
upper to sole (see page 123).
Weave in any loose ends. Blanket
stitch across toe ends of feet
using orange.

jester bootees

An original design that is great for a Christmas baby. Jingling bells and a pointed edging finish them off beautifully, while a ribbon tie keeps them on feet.

SIZE
To fit baby of 6–9 months

MATERIALS
Jaeger merino dk
1¾oz (50g) balls each of
red (A)	1
cream (B)	1
1 pair of US 3 (3¼mm) needles
39in (100cm) of ribbon
2 small bells

BEFORE YOU START
Gauge (Tension)
24sts and 32 rows = 4in (10cm) square over stockinette (stocking) stitch using US 3 (3¼mm) needles.

Abbreviations
s2 = slip next 2sts purlwise.
See also page 126.

BASIC KNIT
First bootee
Sole
Using A, cast on 41sts.
ROW 1: *inc, k18, inc* twice, k1.
ROWS 2–3: knit.
ROW 4: *inc, k20, inc* twice, k1.
ROWS 5–6: knit.
ROW 7: *inc, k22, inc* twice, k1. *(53sts)*
ROWS 8–9: knit.
ROW 10: purl.
ROW 11: k1, *yo, k2tog* to end.
ROW 12: purl.
ROWS 13–14: as rows 9 –10.
ROW 15: make hem, fold work at row of holes and knit together, 1 stitch from needle and 1 stitch from row 9, across row.
ROW 16: k2tog, k51.

Sides
ROW 17: knit 26A, 26B.
ROW 18: using B, k24, inc, k1, yf, using A, inc, k25.
ROW 19: knit 27A, 27B.
ROW 20: using B, k25, inc, k1, yf, using A, inc, k26.
ROWS 21–28: inc as set. *(64sts)*
ROW 29: knit 32A, 16B, turn.
ROW 30: using B, s1, k13, inc, k1, yf, using A, inc, k15, turn.
ROW 31: s1, k16A, k13B, turn.
ROW 32: using B, s1, k10, inc, k1, yf, using A, inc, k12, turn. *(68sts)*
ROW 33: s1, k13A, k10B, turn.
ROW 34: s1, k9B, yf, k10A, turn.
ROW 35: s1, k9A, k6B, turn.
ROW 36: s1, k5B, yf, k6A, turn.
ROW 37: s1, k5A, k2B, turn.
ROW 38: s1, k1B, yf, k2A, s1, turn.

ROW 39: using A, k2tog, k1, using B, k1, s1, k1, psso.
ROW 40: k2B, yf, k2A, s2, turn.
ROW 41: using A, k3tog, k1, using B, k1, s1, k2tog, psso, turn.
ROW 42–53: as rows 40–41 six times.
ROW 54: as row 40.
ROW 55: using A, k3tog, k1, using B, k1, s1, k2tog, psso, k15. *(34sts)*
ROW 56: purl 17B, 17A.
ROWS 57–58: 17sts of each color in stockinette (stocking) stitch.
ROW 59: using A, *k2, yo, k2tog* four times k1, using B *k2, yo, k2tog* four times, k1.
ROWS 60–63: 17sts of each color in stockinette (stocking) stitch.
ROW 64: knit 17B, 17A.
ROW 65: bind (cast) off.

Trim
Using A, cast on 2sts.
ROW 1: inc, k1.
ROW 2: k1, p1, inc.
ROW 3: inc, k1, p1, k1.
ROW 4: k1, p1, k1, p2tog.
ROW 5: k2tog, p1, k1.
ROW 6: k1, p2tog.
Repeat rows 1–6 four times.
Change to B. Work rows 1–6 five times.
Bind (cast) off.

Second bootee
Sole
As for first bootee.

Sides
Work as for first bootee, but reverse colors, eg:
ROW 1: knit 26B, 26A

FINISHING
Join sole and back seam. Weave in any loose ends. Attach trim around ankle just below bind (cast) off. Cut ribbon in half, thread through eyelets and tie in bow. Stitch bell to each toe (see page 123).

polka-dot shoes
Comic-book shoes to make the most of a tiny girl's toes. Red and white is a classic color combination, but they also look good in complementary colorways; try blue and yellow, for example.

SIZE
To fit baby of 6–9 months

MATERIALS
Rowan cotton glacé
1¾oz (50g) ball of
    red (M)   1
Small amount of white (C)
1 pair of US 2 (3mm) needles
2 small buttons

BEFORE YOU START
Gauge (Tension)
26sts and 32 rows = 4in (10cm)
square over Fair Isle using US 2
(3mm) needles.

Abbreviations
See page 126.

BASIC KNIT
Sole
Using M, cast on 42sts.
ROW 1: k1, inc, k16, inc, k4, inc,
k16, inc, k1.
ROW 2 & ALT ROWS: knit.
ROW 3: k2, inc, k17, inc, k4, inc,
k17, inc, k2.
ROW 5: k3, inc, k18, inc, k4, inc,
k18, inc, k3.
ROW 7: k4, inc, k19, inc, k4, inc,
k19, inc, k4.
ROW 9: k5, inc, k20, inc, k4, inc,
k20, inc, k5. *(62sts)*

Side of shoe
Change to stockinette (stocking)
stitch.
ROW 1: M.
ROW 2: *2C, 4M* to last
2sts, 2C.
ROWS 3–4: 3C, *2M, 4C* to last
5sts, 2M, 3C.
ROW 5: as row 2.
ROW 6: M.
ROW 7: 3M, *2C, 4M* to last
5sts, 2C, 3M.
ROWS 8–9: 2M, *4C, 2M* to end.
ROW 10: as row 7.

Start instep
ROW 11: using M, k35, s1, k1,
psso, turn.
ROW 12: s1, 3M, 2C, 3M,
p2tog, turn.
ROW 13: s1, 2M, 4C, 2M, s1, k1,
psso, turn.
ROW 14: s1, 2M, 4C, 2M,
p2tog, turn.
ROW 15: s1, 3M, 2C, 3M, s1, k1,
psso, turn.
ROW 16: s1, 8M, p2tog, turn.
ROW 17: s1, 8M, s1, k1, psso, turn.
ROW 18: as row 16.
ROWS 19–22: as rows 17–18 twice.
ROW 23: s1, k8, s1, k1, psso, k19.
ROW 24: k28, k2tog, knit 19.
ROW 25: bind (cast) off.

Ankle strap
Join heel and underfoot seam.
Weave in any loose ends.
Cast on 7sts, with RS facing, pick
up and knit 14sts from heel
(7sts from each side of heel
seam), cast on 7sts.
ROW 1: knit.
ROW 2: knit to last 4sts, k2tog,
yo, k2.
ROW 3: knit.
ROW 4: bind (cast) off.

Bow
Cast on 20sts. Knit 13 rows.
Bind (cast) off.

Second shoe
Make second shoe to match.

FINISHING
Stitch ends of bow together and
fold in half with seam at center
back. Run a gathering thread
vertically through center of bow
and pull tight, then wrap yarn
several times around center of the
bow to cover gathering thread.
Stitch bow to front of shoe (see
photograph). Stitch on buttons
(see page 123).

simple shoes
A wonderfully easy design to knit, these shoes can be embellished in dozens of different ways to co-ordinate with any outfit or to suit any occasion.

❶ Rose shoe
Store-bought embellishments really come into their own here. Experiment with different colors and styles.

❷ Sequin shoe
Glamorous girls will love these sequinned shoes. Choose the brightest colors and co-ordinating buttons.

❸ Watermelon shoe
Use cotton embroidery thread and simple stitches to embroider a motif onto the toes of a pair of shoes.

❹ Star shoe
So simple a child could do it. The embroidery on this shoe is an arrangement of straight stitches and French knots.

simple shoes cont

SIZE
To fit baby of 3–6 months

MATERIALS
Choose between
❶ **Rose shoe**
Rowan 4 ply cotton
1¾oz (50g) ball of
   pale green   1
Silk rose and bow

❷ **Sequin shoe**
Rowan-4 ply cotton
1¾oz (50g) ball of
   purple   1
Sequin strip and heart motif

❸ **Watermelon shoe**
Rowan 4 ply cotton
1¾oz (50g) ball of
   pale pink   1
Pink, green and black
   embroidery thread

❹ **Star shoe**
Rowan 4 ply cotton
1¾oz (50g) ball of
   pale blue   1
Blue embroidery thread

1 pair of US 2 (2¾mm) needles
Safety pin
2 small buttons

BEFORE YOU START
Gauge (Tension)
28sts and 38 rows = 4in
(10cm) square over stockinette
(stocking) stitch using US 2
(2¾mm) needles.

Abbreviations
See page 126

BASIC KNIT
Right shoe
Sole
Cast on 24sts and work in seed
(moss) stitch.
Inc each end of rows 2, 4, 6,
and 8. *(32sts)*
Work 3 rows. Dec each end of
rows 12, 14, 16 and 18. *(24sts)*
ROW 19: seed (moss) to end, cast
on 8sts.

Upper
ROW 1: knit.
ROW 2: inc, purl to end.
ROWS 3–8: as rows 1–2 three times.
ROW 9: knit.
ROW 10: inc, p14, seed (moss) 21.
ROW 11: seed (moss) 21, k16.
ROW 12: inc, p15, seed (moss) 21.
(38sts)
ROW 13: bind (cast) off 12sts, seed
(moss) 3, bind (cast) off 4sts,
moss 2, k17.
ROW 14: p17, seed (moss) 2, leave
3sts on safety pin.
ROW 15: seed (moss) 2, k17.
ROWS 16–25: as rows 14–15
five times.
ROW 26: p17, seed (moss) 2, cast
on 19sts.
ROW 27: seed (moss) 21, k17.

ROW 28: p2tog, p15, moss
(seed) 21.
ROW 29: seed (moss) 21, k16.
ROW 30: p2tog, purl to end.
ROWS 31–38: work in stockinette
(stocking) stitch, dec beg of each
purl row.
ROW 39: bind (cast) off.

Strap
Place 3sts from safety pin
onto needle.
ROW 1: inc, inc, k1.
ROWS 2–15: seed (moss) stitch.
ROW 16: seed (moss) 2, bind
(cast) off 1, seed (moss) 2.
ROW 17: seed (moss) 2, yo, seed
(moss) 2.
ROWS 18–20: seed (moss) stitch.
ROW 21: bind (cast) off.

Left shoe
Sole
As for right shoe.

Upper
Reverse stockinette (stocking)
stitch, eg:
ROW 1: purl.
ROW 2: inc, knit to end.
ROW 10: inc, k14, seed (moss) 21.

FINISHING
Join heel seam. Carefully fit upper
to sole, easing fullness around toe
area, and stitch into position.
Weave in any loose ends. Stitch
on buttons (see page 123).

❶ **Rose shoe**
Stitch silk rose (available from
good haberdashery and craft
shops) to front and bow to heel
of shoe.

❷ **Sequin shoe**
Stitch sequin strip around rim of
shoe and across strap. Stitch
sequin heart motif to toe of shoe.

❸ **Watermelon shoe**
Using satin stitch, embroider
simple watermelon shape (see
photograph on page 70) on toe of
shoe. Add black French knots for
seeds.

❹ **Star shoe**
Using straight stitch, embroider a
star on toe of shoe with French
knots at the ends of each stitch
(see photograph on page 70).

ladybird shoes

You are sure to smile when you see your baby's feet in these colorful, fun shoes. They are bold and bright with a simple textured sole for added detail.

SIZE
To fit baby of 3–6 months

MATERIALS
Rowan cotton glacé
1¾oz (50g) balls each of
  black (A)   1
  red (B)   1
1 pair of US 2 (2¾mm) needles

BEFORE YOU START
Gauge (Tension)
26sts and 34 rows = 4in (10cm) square over Fair Isle using US 2 (2¾mm) needles.

Abbreviations
See page 126.

BASIC KNIT
Sole
Start at heel end. Using A, cast on 3sts and work in seed (moss) stitch. Inc each end of rows 2, 3, 5, 6 and 8. (13sts)
Cont without shaping to completion of row 36. Dec each end of next and every alt row to 5sts.
NEXT ROW: purl.
Change to stocking (stockinette) stitch.

Upper
ROW 1: using B, inc in 2sts, 1A, using B, inc in 2sts. (9sts)
ROW 2: 4B, 1A, 4B.
ROW 3: 1B, inc B, inc B, 1B ,1A, inc B, inc B, 2B. (13sts)
ROW 4: 6B, 1A, 6B.
Row 5: 2B, inc B, inc B, 2B, 1A, 1B, inc B, inc B, 3B. (17sts)
ROW 6: 3B, 2A, 3B, 1A, 3B, 2A, 3B.
ROW 7: 3B, inc A, 2A, 2B, 1A, 2B, 1A, inc A, 1A, 3B. (19sts)
ROW 8: 4B, 2A, 3B, 1A, 3B, 2A, 4B.
ROW 9: 9B, 1A, 9B.
ROW 10: *2B, inc B* twice, 3B, 1A, *2B, inc B* twice, 3B. (23sts)
ROW 11: work ladybird pattern following instructions and chart: 11B, 1A, 11B.
ROW 12: 11B, 1A, 11B.
ROW 13: 3B, 2A, 6B, 1A, 6B, 2A, 3B.
ROWS 14–15: 2B, 4A, 5B, 1A, 5B, 4A, 2B.
ROW 16: as row 13.
ROW 17: 7B, 2A, 2B, 1A, 2B, 2A, 7B.
ROWS 18–19: 6B, 4A, 1B, 1A, 1B, 4A, 6B.
ROW 20: as row 17.
ROWS 21–24: 11B, 1A, 11B.
ROW 25: 10B, bind (cast) off 3sts, 10B.
On 10sts
ROW 26: 3B, 2A, 5B.
ROW 27: 1B, 2togB, 1B 4A, 2B.
ROW 28: 2B, 4A, 3B.
ROW 29: 1B, 2togB, 1B, 2A, 3B.
ROW 30: B.
ROW 31: 1B, 2togB, 5B. (7sts)
ROWS 32–34: B.

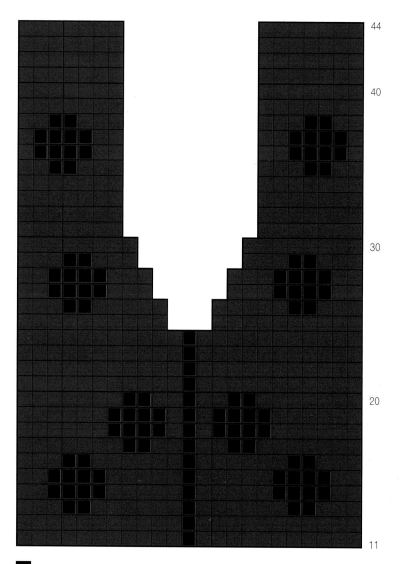

■ A

 B

ROW 35: **3B, 2A, 2B.**
ROW 36: **1B, 4A, 2B.**
ROW 37: **2B, 4A, 1B.**
ROW 38: **2B, 2A, 3B.**
ROWS 39–44: **B.**
ROW 45: **bind (cast) off.**
Rejoin yarn to remaining sts at center front.
ROW 26: **WS facing, 5B, 2A, 3B.**
ROW 27: **2B, 4A, 1B, s1, k1B, psso, 1B.**
Cont decs as set and work to match first side.

Trim
Using A, pick up 3sts in every 4 rows around ankle.
Bind (cast) off.

Second shoe
Make second shoe to match.

FINISHING
Join heel seam, pin to heel end of sole. Carefully pin upper to sole, easing any excess around toe area and stitch into position (see page 123). Weave in any loose ends.

lace and diamond bootees
Classic bootees that combine different textures, these are perfect for a contemporary christening or a wedding as they are pretty, but not too frilly.

SIZE
To fit baby of 6–9 months

MATERIALS
Rowan cotton glace
1¾oz (50g) ball of
   cream   1
1 pair of US 3 (3¼mm) needles
30in (76cm) of ribbon

BEFORE YOU START
Gauge (Tension)
24sts and 30 rows = 4in
(10cm) square over stockinette
(stocking) stitch using US 3
(3¼mm) needles.

Abbreviations
See page 126.

BASIC KNIT
Cuff
Cast on 49sts.
ROW 1: *k1, yo, k4, s1, k2tog, psso, k4, yo* four times, k1.
ROW 2 & ALT ROWS: purl.
ROW 3: *k2, yo, k3, s1, k2tog, psso, k3, yo, k1* four times, k1.
ROW 5: *k3, yo, k2, s1, k2tog, psso, k2, yo, k2* four times, k1.
ROW 7: *k4, yo, k1, s1, k2tog, psso, k1, yo, k3* four times, k1.
ROW 9: *k5, s1, k2tog, psso, k4* 4 times, k1. (41sts)
ROW 10: *p2tog, p8* four times, p1. (37sts)
Change to k1, p1 rib, work 7 rows.
NEXT ROW: k1 *k1, yo, k2tog* to end.
Change to stockinette (stocking) stitch. Work 3 rows, starting with a purl row.

Divide for top of foot
K25, turn, p13, turn.
On 13sts, work 4 rows in stockinette (stocking) stitch.
ROW 5: k6, p1, k6.
ROW 6: p5, k3, p5.
ROW 7: k4, p5, k4.
ROW 8: p3, k7, p3.
ROW 9: k2, p9, k2.
ROW 10: as row 8.
ROW 11: as row 7.
ROW 12: as row 6.
ROW 13: as row 5.
ROWS 14–16: stockinette (stocking) stitch. Break yarn.
With RS facing, (12sts on needle), pick up and knit 13sts along side of foot, 13sts from toe, 13sts from side of foot and 12sts from needle. (63sts)
Knit 11 rows.

Shape sole
ROW 1: *k1, k2tog, k26, k2tog* twice, k1.
ROW 2: k1, k2tog, knit to last 3sts, k2tog, k1.
ROW 3: *k1, k2tog, k23, k2tog* twice, k1.
ROW 4: as row 2.
ROW 5: *k1, k2tog, k20, k2tog* twice, k1.
ROW 6: bind (cast) off.

Second bootee
Make second bootee to match.

FINISHING
Join leg seam and under foot seam. Weave in any loose ends. Cut ribbon in half, thread through eyelets and tie in bow (see page 123).

fish bootees

A panel of little goldfish swim happily around a baby's toes in this design. The simple motif in bright colors stands out boldly on the dark background.

SIZE
To fit baby of 0–3 months

MATERIALS
Jaeger merino dk
1¾oz (50g) ball of
   navy (M)   1
Small amounts of yellow (A)
   and orange (B)
1 pair each of US 3 (3¼mm) and
US 5 (3¾mm) needles

BEFORE YOU START
Gauge (Tension)
24sts and 32 rows = 4in
(10cm) square over stockinette
(stocking) stitch using US 5
(3¾mm) needles.

Abbreviations
See page 126.

BASIC KNIT
Cuff
Using US 3 (3¼mm) needles and
B, cast on 32sts.
Change to M and work 21 rows in
k1, p1 rib.
Change to US 5 (3¾mm) needles
and stockinette (stocking) stitch.
Work 4 rows.

Divide for top of foot
K21, turn, p10, turn.
On 10sts, work 14 rows.
Break yarn.
With RS facing, *(11sts on needle)*,
rejoin M and pick up 9sts along
side of foot, 10sts from toe, 9sts
along side of foot and 11sts on
needle. *(50sts)*
Work in stockinette (stocking)
stitch as folls, starting with a
purl row:
ROW 1: place fish motif following
instructions and chart: A.
ROW 2: M.
ROW 3: *1M, 2B, 4M, 3B, 2M*
twice, 2M, *2M, 3B, 4M, 2B,
1M* twice.

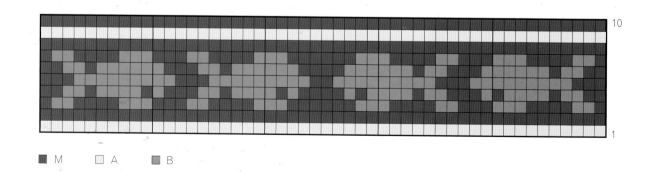

■ M   □ A   ■ B

ROW 4: *2M, 2B, 1M, 4B, 1M, 1B, 1M* twice, 2M, *1M, 1B, 1M, 4B, 1M, 2B, 2M* twice.

ROW 5: *3M, 9B* twice, 2M, *9B, 3M* twice.

ROW 6: *2M, 2B, 1M, 6B, 1M* twice, 2M, *1M, 6B, 1M, 2B, 2M* twice.

ROW 7: as row 3. Break B.

ROW 8: M.

ROW 9: A. Break A.

ROW 10: M.

Shape sole

ROW 1: knit.

ROW 2: *k1, k2tog, k19, k2tog, k1* twice.

ROW 3: knit.

ROW 4: *k1, k2tog, k17, k2tog, k1* twice.

ROW 5: *k1, k2tog, k15, k2tog, k1* twice.

ROW 6: knit.

ROW 7: bind (cast) off.

Second bootee

Make second bootee to match.

FINISHING

Join leg seam and under foot seam (see page 123). Weave in any loose ends.

entrelac socks

These socks are have entrelac cuffs and are a more challenging design for the experienced knitter to try.

SIZE
To fit baby of 3–6 months

MATERIALS
Jaeger merino 4 ply
1¾oz (50g) balls of each
cream (M)	1
red (C)	1
1 pair of US 2 (3mm) needles

BEFORE YOU START
Gauge (Tension)
28sts and 38 rows = 4in (10cm) square over stockinette (stocking) stitch using US 2 (3mm) needles.

Abbreviations
See page 126

BASIC KNIT
Cuff
Using C, cast on 56sts and knit 1 row.
Start entrelac
ROW 1: k3, s1, k1, psso, turn, p4.
◆ROWS 2–3: as row 1.
ROW 4: *k3, s1, k1, psso* twice, turn, p4.◆
Repeat ◆ to ◆ along row, casting (binding) off 4sts at end of last repeat.
With WS facing and using M, pick up 4sts purlwise along a, (see fig 5, page 127), turn, k4.
*ROWS 1–3: p3, p2tog, turn, k4.
ROW 4: p3, p2tog, pick up 4sts purlwise along a, (see fig 5, page 127), turn k4.*
Repeat * to * along row. Work 5 rows stockinette (stocking) stitch on last 4 sts. Bind (cast) off.
With RS facing and using C, pick up 4sts along b (see fig 6, page 127), turn, p4.
◆ROWS 1–3: k3, s1, k1, psso, turn, p4.
ROW 4: *k3, s1, k1, psso* twice, turn, p4.◆
Repeat ◆ to ◆ along row. Work 6 rows in stockinette (stocking) stitch on last 4 sts. Break C.
WS facing, using M *p4, pick up 3sts along (a) see page 127* to end. (49sts)
NEXT ROW: *k2, k2tog, k3* to end. (42sts)

Start rib patt
ROW 1: WS facing *k1, p4, k1* to end.
ROW 2: *p1, k4, p1* to end.
ROW 3: *k1, p1, k2, p1, k1* to end.
ROW 4: *p1, k1, p2, k1, p1* to end.
ROWS 5–16: as rows 1–4 three times.
ROW 17: as row 1. Break M.

Work instep
Slip 13sts, using M, *k4, p2* twice, k4, turn.
On 16sts, work 19 rows in patt. Break M.

Work toe
Using C, k2, k2tog, k3, k2tog, k3, s1, k1, psso, k2. (13sts)
Work 3 rows in seed (moss) stitch (every row *k1, p1* to last stitch, k1). Dec each end of next and foll 4th row. (9sts)
Work 3 rows. Break C.

Work heel and foot
Slip all sts onto 1 needle, RS facing, using C, k13, pick up and knit 11 sts along instep, 6sts along toe, seed (moss) 9sts from needle, pick up and knit 6sts along toe, 11sts along instep, k13sts from needle (69sts)
Work in seed (moss) stitch, shaping rows only given.
ROW 5: seed (moss) 27, p3tog, seed (moss) 9, p3tog, seed (moss) 27.
ROW 9: seed (moss) 26, s1, k2tog, psso, seed (moss) 7, s1, k2tog, psso, seed (moss) 26.
ROW 13: seed (moss) 25, p3tog, seed (moss) 5, p3tog, seed (moss) 25.
ROW 16: seed (moss) 2, *s1, k2tog, psso, seed (moss) 19, s1, k2tog, psso*, seed (moss) 3, *to* again, seed (moss) 2.
Row 18: *k1, p3tog, seed (moss) 17, p3tog* twice, k1.

Second sock
Make second sock to match.

FINISHING
Join leg and underfoot seam (see page 123). Weave in any loose ends.

fair isle shoes

Fair isle fans will love these ankle-strap shoes, which look good in pastel shades, as well as in the darker, bolder colors shown here.

SIZE
To fit baby of 3–6 months

MATERIALS
Rowan cotton glacé
1¾oz (50g) ball of
    dark blue (M)   1
Small amounts of yellow (A),
    red (B) and green (C)
1 pair of US 2 (2¾mm) needles.
2 small buttons

BEFORE YOU START
Gauge (Tension)
26sts and 34 rows = 4in (10cm)
square over Fair Isle using US 2
(2¾mm) needles.

Abbreviations
See page 126.

BASIC KNIT
Sole
Using M, cast on 19sts and work
in seed (moss) stitch.
Inc each end of rows 2, 4 and 6.
(25sts)
Work 2 rows. Dec each end of
rows 9, 11 and 13. *(19sts)*
ROW 14: moss to end, cast on
6sts. *(25sts)*

Upper
Change to stockinette (stocking)
stitch and work Fair Isle following
instructions and chart (starting
with a knit row):
ROW 1: *1M, 1A* to last st, 1M.
ROW 2: M inc, purl to end.
ROW 3: 1M, *1B, 2M, 1C, 2M* to
last st, 1B.
ROW 4: inc B, *1B, 1C, 1A, 1C, 1B,
1A* to last st, 1B.

ROW 5: as row 3 to last 2sts,
1B, 1M.
ROW 6: as row 2.
ROW 7: *1M, 1A* to end.
ROW 8: M inc p10, *k1, p1* to
last st, k1.
ROW 9: seed (moss) 18M, knit 1M,
1B, 2M, 1C, 2M, 1B, 2M, 1C.
ROW 10: purl inc A, 1C, 1B, 1A, 1B,
1C, 1A, 1C, 1B, 1A, 1B, using M,
p1, k1 to end.
ROW 11: bind (cast) off 15sts, *p1,
k1* twice, knit 1B, 2M, 1C, 2M, 1B,
2M, 1C, 1M.
ROW 12: using M, p13, k1, p1.
ROW 13: using M, *p1, k1* twice,
knit *1A, 1M* to last st, 1A.
ROW 14: as row 12.
ROW 15: using M, *p1, k1* twice,
knit 1B, 2M, 1C, 2M, 1B, 2M,
1C, 1M.
ROW 16: purl *1C, 1A, 1C, 1B, 1A,
1B* twice, using M, p1, k1, p1,
cast on 15sts.
ROW 17: seed (moss) 18M, knit 1M,
1B, 2M, 1C, 2M, 1B, 2M, 2togC.
ROW 18: using M, p11, moss
(seed) 18.
ROW 19: knit *1M, 1A* to last 3sts,
1M, 2togA.
ROW 20: M.
ROW 21: as row 3 to last 3sts,
1B, 2togM.
ROW 22: *1B, 1A, 1B, 1C, 1A, 1C*
to last 3sts, 1B, 1A, 1B.
ROW 23: as row 3 to last 2sts,
2togB.
ROW 24: M.
ROW 25: *1M, 1A* to last
2sts, 2togM.
ROW 26: M.
ROW 27: bind (cast) off.

Second bootee
Make second shoe to match.

FINISHING
Join heel seam. Carefully fit upper
to sole, easing fullness around toe
area, and stitch into position.
Weave in any loose ends.

Strap
Using M, cast on 8sts, with RS of
shoe facing, pick up and knit
10sts from heel (5sts from each
side of heel seam), cast on 8sts.
(26sts)
ROW 1: *k1, p1* to end.
ROW 2: *p1, k1* to last 4sts,
p2tog, yo, p1, k1.
ROW 3: as row 1.
ROW 4: bind (cast) off.
Sew on button (see page 123).

■ M, knit on RS
   purl on WS

■ M, purl on RS
   knit on WS

□ A

■ B

■ C

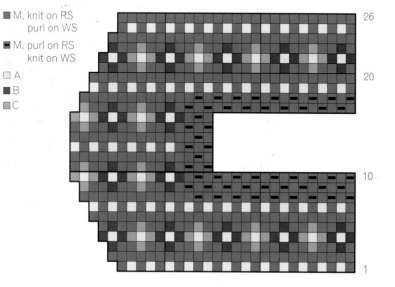

26

20

10

1

roll-top bootees

These bootees are a great, simple shape and the modern roll-top edging in a contrast color complements the simple embellishment.

roll-top bootees cont

SIZE
To fit baby of 0–3(3–6) months

MATERIALS
Jaeger merino 4 ply
1¾oz (50g) ball of
   navy (M)   1
Small amount of red (C)
1 pair of US 2 (3mm) needles

BEFORE YOU START
Gauge (Tension)
28sts and 38 rows = 4in (10cm)
square over stockinette (stocking)
stitch using US 2 (3mm) needles.

Abbreviations
See page 126.

BASIC KNIT
Cuff
Using C, cast on 41sts and
work 10 rows in stockinette
(stocking) stitch.
Change to M and work 6 rows.
ROW 7: k2, *yo, k2tog, k2* nine
times, yo, k2tog, k1.
Work 3 more rows.

Divide for top of foot
K28 turn, p15 turn.
On 15sts, work 16(22) rows.
Break yarn.
With RS facing, (13sts on needle),
rejoin M and pick up 11(17)sts
along side of foot, 15sts from toe,
11(17)sts along side of foot and
13sts on needle. (63:75sts)
Knit 13 rows.

Shape sole
ROW 1: k1, *k2tog, k25(31),
k2tog* k3, *to* again, k1.
ROW 2: k26(32,) k2tog, k3, k2tog,
k26(32).
ROW 3: k1, *k2tog, k22(28),
k2tog* k3, *to* again, k1.
ROW 4: k23(29), k2tog, k3, k2tog,
k23(29).
ROW 5: k1, *k2tog, k19(25),
k2tog* k3, *to* again, k1.
ROW 6: bind (cast) off.

Make ties
Using C, cut six 18in (46cm)
lengths of yarn. Knot together at
one end. With two strands for
each section, plait to end and knot
to secure.

Second bootee
Make second bootee to match.

FINISHING
Join leg seam and under foot
seam. Weave in any loose ends.
Make French knots around
garter stitch edge and embroider
straight stitch star on toe (see
photograph). Thread ties
through eyelets and tie in bow
(see page 123).

tiger bootees Stylish bootees for wild little ones.
Cool cotton yarn makes them comfortable in summer, as well as fashionable.

SIZE
To fit baby of 3–6 months

MATERIALS
Rowan cotton glacé
1¾oz (50g) balls each of
    black (A)   1
    yellow (B)   1
1 pair of of US 2 (2¾mm) needles

BEFORE YOU START
Gauge (Tension)
26sts and 34 rows = 4in
(10cm) square over stockinette
(stocking) stitch using US 2
(2¾mm) needles.

Abbreviations
See page 126.

BASIC KNIT
Sole
Start at heel end. Using A, cast on
3sts and work in seed (moss)
stitch. Inc each end of rows 2, 3,
5, 6 and 8. *(13sts)*
Cont without shaping to
completion of row 36. Dec each
end of next and every alt row to
5sts.
NEXT ROW: purl.

Upper
ROW 1: using B, inc in 2sts, k1, inc
in 2sts. *(9sts)*
ROW 2: purl.
ROW 3: k1, *inc in next 2sts, k2*
twice. *(13sts)*
ROW 4: purl.
Cont in stockinette (stocking)
stitch.
ROW 5: k2, inc in next 2sts, k4, inc
in next 2sts, k3. *(17sts)*
ROW 6: 3A, 11B, 3A.
ROW 7: 2A, inc A, 3A, 5B, 3A, inc
A, 2A. *(19sts)*
ROW 8: 6A, 7B, 6A.
ROW 9: 2A, 15B, 2A.
ROW 10: using B, *p2, inc* twice,
p6, *inc, p2* twice, p1. *(23sts)*
ROW 11: work tiger pattern
following instructions and
chart: B.
ROW 12: 4A, 15B, 4A.
ROW 13: 10A, 3B, 10A.
ROW 14: 8A, 7B, 8A.
ROW 15: 4A, 15B, 4A.
ROWS 16–17: B.
ROW 18: 1A, 21B, 1A.
ROW 19: 4A, 15B, 4A.
ROW 20: 7A, 9B, 7A.
ROW 21: 10A, 3B, 10A.
ROW 22: 6A, 11B, 6A.
ROW 23: 3A, 17B, 3A.
ROW 24: B.
ROW 25: 10B, bind (cast) off
3sts, 10B.
On 10sts
ROW 26: 3A, 7B.
ROW 27: 1B, 2togB, 2B, 5A.
ROW 28: 2A, 7B.
ROW 29: 1B, 2togB, 6B.
ROW 30: B.
ROW 31: 1B, 2togB, 2B, 3A. *(7sts)*

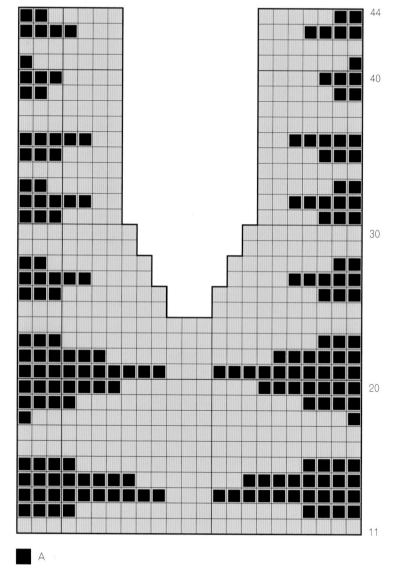

■ A
▨ B

ROW 32: **5A, 2B.**
ROW 33: **5B, 2A.**
ROW 34: **B.**
ROW 35: **4B, 3A.**
ROW 36: **5A, 2B.**
ROWS 37–38: **B.**
ROW 39: **5B, 2A.**
ROW 40: **3A, 4B.**
ROW 41: **6B, 1A.**
ROW 42: **B.**
ROW 43: **3B, 4A.**
ROW 44: **2A, 5B.**
ROW 45: **bind (cast) off.**
Rejoin yarn to remaining sts at center front.
ROW 26: **WS facing, 7B, 3A.**
ROW 27: **5A, 2B, s1, 1B, psso, 1B.**
Cont decs as set and work to match first side.

Cuff

With RS facing and using A, pick up 35sts around ankle.
Work 26 rows in k1, p1 rib.
WS facing, change to B and knit 1 row. Bind (cast) off.

Second bootee

Make second bootee to match.

FINISHING

Join cuff and heel seam, pin to heel end of sole. Carefully pin upper to sole, easing any excess around toe area, and stitch into position (see page 123). Weave in any loose ends.

heart socks
This traditional fair isle design looks so sweet on tiny socks. You can try knitting it in pastel shades for a more subtle look, or vibrant contrasting colors for a funky feel.

SIZE
To fit baby of 3–6 months

MATERIALS
Jaeger merino 4 ply
1¾oz (50g) ball each of
   navy (M)   1
   red (C)   1
4 double-ended US 2
(3mm) needles

BEFORE YOU START
Gauge (Tension)
28sts and 38 rows = 4in (10cm)
square over stockinette (stocking)
stitch using US 2 (3mm) needles.

Abbreviations
See page 126.

BASIC KNIT
Note: place marker at beginning of round.

Cuff
Using C, cast on 36sts
(12sts on 3 needles).
Change to M and knit 1 round.
Work 4 rounds in *k1, p1* to end.
Work heart pattern following instructions and chart (all rounds knit):
ROUND 1: C.
ROUNDS 2–3: M.

ROUND 4: *1M, 2C* to end.
ROUND 5: *1M, 5C* to end.
ROUNDS 6–7: *2M, 3C, 1M* to end.
ROUND 8: *3M, 1C, 2M* to end.
ROUNDS 9–10: M.
ROUND 11: C.
ROUNDS 12–13: M.
ROUNDS 14: *1C, 2M* to end.
ROUNDS 15–16: M.
Rounds 1–16 form patt repeat.
Work rounds 1–16 again.

Start heel
Using C, k17, turn, p15, turn.
On 15sts, work 6 rows in stockinette (stocking) stitch.

Shape heel
ROW 1: k9, turn.
ROW 2: s1, p2, turn.
ROW 3: s1, k1, s1, k1, psso, k1, turn.
ROW 4: s1, p2, p2tog, p1, turn.
ROW 5: s1, k3, s1, k1, psso, k1, turn.
ROW 6: s1, p4, p2tog, p1, turn.
ROW 7: s1, k5, s1, k1, psso, turn.
ROW 8: s1, p6, p2tog, p1.
Break yarn.
Using C, pick up and knit 6sts along heel, 9sts from needle, 6sts along heel, k19.
Cont as folls:
ROUND 1: using M, k1, s1, k1, psso, k19, k2tog, k18.
ROUND 2: using M, k1, s1, k1, psso, k17, k2tog, k18.
ROUND 3: 1M, s1, 1C, psso, *1C, 1M, 1C* five times, 2togC *1M, 2C* six times.
Cont in patt, working rounds 4–16 then 1–10 again. Break M.

Shape toe
Using C,
ROUND 1: knit.
Round 2: *k2tog, k14, s1, k1, psso* twice.
ROUND 3: knit.
ROUND 4: *k2tog, k12, s1, k1, psso* twice.
ROUND 5: knit.
ROUND 6: *k2tog, k10, s1, k1, psso* twice.
ROUND 7: knit.
ROUND 8: *k2tog, k8, s1, k1, psso* twice.
ROUND 9: knit.
ROUND 10: bind (cast) off.

Second sock
Make second sock to match.

FINISHING
Join toe seam (see page 123).
Weave in any loose ends.

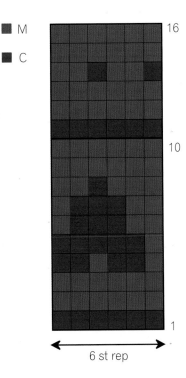

■ M

■ C

16

10

1

6 st rep

chunky ankle-strap shoes
These little shoes knit up very quickly and show off the thickness of the yarn. The wooden buttons add to the rustic feel.

SIZE
To fit baby of 6–9 months

MATERIALS
Rowan polar
3½oz (100g) ball of
    ice blue   1
1 pair of US 6 (4mm) needles
2 small buttons

BEFORE YOU START
Gauge (Tension)
20sts and 38 rows = 4in (10cm) over garter stitch using US 6 (4mm) needles.

Abbreviations
See page 126.

BASIC KNIT
Sole
Cast on 14sts. Working in garter stitch, inc each end of rows 2, 4 and 6. Work row 7. Dec each end of rows 8, 10 and 12.
Bind (cast) off.

Upper
Cast on 19sts. Working in garter stitch, inc beg of rows 2, 4, 6, 8 and 10 (toe end).
ROW 11: bind (cast) off 11sts, knit to end.
ROWS 12–26: knit.
ROW 27: cast on 11sts, k24.
Dec beg rows 28, 30, 32, 34 and 36.
Bind (cast) off.

Strap
Join heel seam on upper. Cast on 10sts, pick up and knit 10sts from back of shoe (5sts each side of heel seam), cast on 10sts.
Knit 1 row.
ROW 2: knit to last 3sts, bind (cast) off 1st, k2.
ROW 3: k2, yo, knit to end.
ROW 4: knit.
ROW 5: bind (cast) off.

Second shoe
Make second shoe to match.

FINISHING
Pin heel seam to center of shaped edge of sole and cast on and bound (cast) off edges of sole end to shoe upper. Run a thread through shaped toe of upper and pull tight until upper fits the shaped (toe) end of sole. Stitch around sole. Weave in any loose ends. Stitch on buttons (see page 123).

star bootees
A simple design and equally easy intarsia motif make these a good project for a knitting beginner.

SIZE
To fit baby of 6–9 months

MATERIALS
Jaeger merino 4 ply
1¾oz (50g) ball of
    dark blue (M)   1
Small amount of yellow (C)
    and green
1 pair of US 2 (3mm) needles

BEFORE YOU START
Gauge (Tension)
28sts and 38 rows = 4in (10cm)
square over stockinette (stocking)
stitch using US 2 (3mm) needles.

Abbreviations
See page 126.

BASIC KNIT
Cuff
Using M, cast on 41sts and work
¾in (2cm) in garter stitch. Change
to stockinette (stocking) stitch,
work 2 rows.
ROW 3: k2, *yo, k2tog, k2* nine
times, yo, k2tog, k1.
Work 3 more rows.

Divide for top of foot
K28 turn, p15 turn.
On 15sts, work 8 rows.
ROW 9: place star motif following
chart: knit 7M, 1C, 7M.

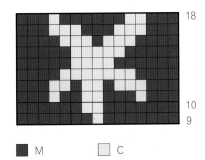

M   C

Work star motif then work 4 more
rows (toe), break yarn.
With RS facing, *(13sts on needle)*,
rejoin M and pick up and knit
16sts along side of foot, 15sts
from toe, 16sts along side of foot
and 13sts on needle. *(73sts)*
Knit 13 rows.

Shape sole
Using M,
ROW 1: k1, *k2tog, k30, k2tog*
k3, *to* again, k1.
ROW 2: k31, k2tog, k3, k2tog, k31.
ROW 3: k1, *k2tog, k27, k2tog*
k3, *to* again, k1.
ROW 4: k28, k2tog, k3,
k2tog, k28.
ROW 5: k1, *k2tog, k24, k2tog*
k3, *to* again, k1.
ROW 6: bind (cast) off.

Second bootee
Make second bootee to match.

FINISHING
Join leg seam and under foot
seam. Weave in any loose ends.
Plait three lengths of green yarn
together to make ties, knotting
ends to secure them. Thread ties
through eyelets and tie in bow
(see page 123).

contrast-edge slippers

These are ideal for a younger baby as they are easy to put on and a fluffy yarn makes them soft and warm.

❶

SIZE
To fit baby of 0–3 months

MATERIALS
Choose from
❶ Pink and green
Rowan kid classic
1¾oz (50g) ball of
    pink (M)   1
Small amount of green (C)

❷ Green and navy
Rowan kid classic
1¾oz (50g) of
    green (M)   1
Small amount of navy (C)

1 pair of US 6 (4mm) needles

BEFORE YOU START
Gauge (Tension)
22sts and 40 rows = 4in (10cm) over garter stitch (every row knit) using US 6 (4mm) needles.

Abbreviations
See page 126.

BASIC KNIT
Sole
Using M, cast on 14sts. Working in garter stitch, inc each end of rows 1, 3, 5 and 7. *(22sts)*
Dec each end of rows 9, 11, 13 and 15. *(14sts)*

Upper
ROW 16: **cast on 5sts** (for heel), k19.
Inc beg rows (toe) 17, 19, 21 and 23. *(23sts)*
ROW 24: **bind (cast) off 12sts, knit to end.**
ROWS 25–35: **knit.**
ROW 36: **cast on 12sts, k23.**
Dec beg rows 37, 39, 41 and 43. *(19sts)*
Bind (cast) off.

Trim
Using C, pick up and knit 12sts from heel to center front, 6sts from center front and 12sts from center front to heel.
Bind (cast) off.

Second slipper
Make second slipper to match.

FINISHING
Join heel seam. Pin upper around sole, easing excess material around toe, and stitch into position (see page 123). Weave in any loose ends.

stripy bootees Firm favorites with me and many other mothers I know, these are great bootees. Not only do the keep a baby's feet warm and snug, but the long, ribbed cuffs mean that they will stay on the most active feet. So if you have a wriggly baby, try knitting this design.

stripy bootees cont

SIZE
To fit baby of 3–6(6–9) months

MATERIALS
Choose from
❶ Dark blue
Rowan dk wool
1¾oz (50g) balls each of
    dark blue (M)   1
    cream (C)   1

❷ Dark pink
Rowan dk wool
1¾oz (50g) balls each of
    dark pink (M)   1
    cream (C)   1

❸ Mid blue
Rowan dk wool
1¾oz (50g) balls each of
    mid blue (M)   1
    cream (C)   1

❹ Pale pink
Rowan dk wool
1¾oz (50g) balls each of
    pale pink (M)   1
    cream (C)   1

1 pair of US 3 (3¼mm) needles

BEFORE YOU START
Gauge (Tension)
26sts and 40 rows = 4in (10cm) square over garter stitch using US 3 (3¼mm) needles.

Abbreviations
See page 126.

BASIC KNIT
Sole
Using M, cast on 43(53)sts.
ROW 1: *inc, k19(24), inc* twice, k1.
ROWS 2–4: knit.
Row 5: *inc, k21(26), inc* twice, k1.
ROWS 6–8: knit.
Row 9: *inc, k23(28), inc* twice, k1.
ROW 10: knit.

Picot edge
Change to C.
ROW 1: knit.
ROW 2: purl.
ROW 3: k1, *yo, k2tog* to end.
ROW 4: purl.
ROWS 5–6: as rows 1–2.
Change to M.
ROW 7: fold work at row of holes and knit together, 1st from needle and 1st from FIRST row of picot, all across row.
ROWS 8–16(20): knit.

Divide for top of foot
ROW 1: using M, k31(36), s1, k1, psso, turn.
ROW 2: using M, k8, k2tog, turn.
ROW 3: using C, k8, s1, k1, psso, turn.
ROW 4: using C, k8, k2tog, turn.
ROWS 5–6: using M, as rows 3–4.
ROWS 7–18(22): as rows 3–6.
Work rows 3–4 again.
NEXT ROW: using M, k9, knit to end.
Knit 3 rows across all stitches.

Cuff
Change to k1, p1 rib.
ROWS 1–8: M.
ROW 9: knit in C.
ROWS 10–28: still in C, work in k1, p1 rib.
ROW 29: purl in M.
Bind (cast) off in M.

Second bootee
Make second bootee to match

FINISHING
Join seam using a flat seam (see page 123). Weave in any loose ends.

cable socks

The simple shape of this design shows off the cabling beautifully and makes it a great project for knitters who prefer single color work.

SIZE
To fit baby of 3–6 months

MATERIALS
Jaeger merino 4 ply
1¾oz (50g) ball of
   cream   1
1 pair of US 2 (3mm) needles
Cable needle

BEFORE YOU START
Gauge (Tension)
28sts and 38 rows = 4in (10cm) square over stockinette (stocking) stitch using US 2 (3mm) needles.

Abbreviations
c4b = slip 2 sts onto cable needle and hold at back of work, k2 from left hand needle, then k2 from cable needle.
See also page 126.

BASIC KNIT
Cuff
Cast on 36sts and work 5 rows in k1, p1 rib.
ROW 6: *rib 3, inc, rib 2* to end. *(42sts)*
Patt as folls:
ROW 1: *k4, p3* to end.
ROW 2: *k2tog, yo, k1, p4* to end.
ROW 3: *c4b, p3* to end.
ROW 4: *k3, p4* to end.
ROW 5: as row 1.
ROW 6: as row 4.
ROWS 7–24: as rows 1–6 three times.
ROWS 25–27: as rows 1–3.

Divide for instep
ROW 28: patt 35, turn,
patt 18, turn.

Work instep
On 18sts, work 22 rows in patt.
ROW 23: *p1, p2tog, p1, k3* twice, p1, p2tog, p1. Break yarn. *(15sts)*

Work heel and foot
Put all sts onto one needle.
With RS facing, k1, k2tog, k4, pick up and knit 20sts along instep, 15sts from needle, 20sts along instep and *k4, k2tog, k1* twice, k3 from needle. *(76sts)*

Cont as folls:
ROW 1 AND ALT ROWS: purl.
ROW 2: k25, s1, k1, psso, k13, k2tog, k34.
ROW 4: k25, s1, k1, psso, k11, k2tog, k34.
ROW 6: k25, s1, k1, psso, k9, k2tog, k34.
ROW 8: k25, s1, k1, psso, k7, k2tog, k34.
ROW 10: k2tog, k22, s1, k2tog, psso, k5, k3tog, k22, s1, k2tog, psso, k6, k2tog.
ROW 12: k2tog, k20, s1, k2tog, psso, k3, k3tog, k20, s1, k2tog, psso, k4, k2tog.
ROW 14: k2tog, k18, s1, k2tog, psso, k1, k3tog, k18, s1, k2tog, psso, k2, k2tog.
ROW 15: purl.
ROW 16: bind (cast) off.

Second sock
Make second sock to match.

FINISHING
Join leg seam; this is NOT center back. Carefully pin underfoot seam, using shapings to mark center heel and toe. Stitch sole seam (see page 123). Weave in any loose ends.

tassel shoes
These shoes look great in primary colors and are really easy to knit – a good design for a novice knitter to try.

SIZE
To fit baby of 0–3 months

MATERIALS
Jaeger merino dk
1¾oz (50g) ball of
   red   1
Small amounts of green, blue
   and yellow
1 pair of US 6 (4mm) needles
2 small buttons

BEFORE YOU START
Gauge (Tension)
22sts and 40 rows = 4in (10cm)
square over garter stitch using
US 6 (4mm) needles.

Abbreviations
See page 126.

BASIC KNIT
Sole
Cast on 32sts.
ROW 1: *k1, inc, k12, inc, k1* twice.
ROW 2 & ALT ROWS: knit.
ROW 3: *k1, inc, k14, inc, k1* twice.
ROW 5: *k1, inc, k16, inc, k1* twice.
ROW 7: *k1, inc, k18, inc, k1* twice.
ROW 9: *k1, inc, k20, inc, k1* twice. (52sts)
ROWS 10–15: knit.

Shape instep
ROW 16: k30, turn.
ROW 17–33: k7, s1, k1, psso, turn. (35sts)
ROW 34: k7, s1, k1, psso, k13.
ROWS 35–37: knit across all sts.
ROW 38: bind (cast) off.

Ankle strap
Join heel and underfoot seam.
Cast on 6sts, with RS facing pick up and knit 12sts from heel (6sts each side of heel seam), cast on 6sts.
ROW 1: knit.
ROW 2: knit to last 4sts, k2tog, yo, k2.
ROW 3: knit.
ROW 4: Bind (cast) off.

Second shoe
Make second shoe to match.

FINISHING
Weave in any loose ends. Cut five 10in (25cm) lengths of blue yarn. Fold in half and, using a crochet hook, push folded ends under a stitch approx ½in (1cm) below center front. Tuck cut ends of yarn through loop and pull tight to make a tassel. Repeat with green and yellow yarn either side of blue yarn. Trim cut ends neatly. Reverse order of colors on second shoe. Sew on buttons (see page 123).

center cable bootees

The central cable on these bootees is easy to knit and a contrast color makes the most of the texture.

SIZE

To fit baby of 3–6 months

MATERIALS

Rowan dk wool
1¾oz (50g) ball of
  mid-blue (M)   1
Small amount of cream (C)
1 pair of US 2 (3mm) needles
Cable needle

BEFORE YOU START

Gauge (Tension)

26sts and 36 rows = 4in (10cm)
square over stockinette (stocking)
stitch using US 2 (3mm) needles.

Abbreviations

c4b = slip 2 sts onto cable
needle and hold at back of work,
k2 from left hand needle, then k2
from cable needle.
See also page 126.

BASIC KNIT

Sole

Start at heel end. Using M, cast
on 2sts and work in seed (moss)
stitch. Inc each end of rows 2, 3,
5, 6 and 8. *(12sts)*
Cont without shaping to completion
of row 36. Dec each end of next
and every alt row to 4sts.
NEXT ROW: purl.

Upper

Change to stocking
(stockinette) stitch.
ROW 1: inc in each stitch. *(8sts)*
ROW 2: 2M, 4C, 2M.
ROW 3: *inc M* twice, 4C, *inc
M* twice. *(12sts)*
ROW 4: 4M, 4C, 4M.
ROW 5: 1M, *inc M* twice, 1M,
c4bC, 1M, *inc M* twice, 1M.
(16sts)
ROW 6: 6M, 4C, 6M.
ROW 7: 3M, inc M, 2M, 4C, 2M,
inc M, 3M. *(18sts)*
ROW 8: 7M, 4C, 7M.
ROW 9: 7M, c4bC, 7M.
ROW 10: *2M, inc M* twice, 1M,
4C, 1M, *inc M, 2M* twice.
(22sts)
ROWS 11–12: 9M, 4C, 9M.
ROW 13: 9M, c4bC, 9M.
ROW 14: as row 12.
ROWS 15–22: as rows 11–14 twice.
ROWS 23–24: as rows 11–12.
ROW 25: 9M, bind (cast) off
4sts, 9M.

On 9sts, using M,
ROW 26: purl.
ROW 27: k1, k2tog, k6.
ROW 28: purl.
ROW 29: k1, k2tog, k5.
ROW 30: purl.
ROWS 31–42: stocking
(stockinette) stitch.
ROW 43: bind (cast) off.
Rejoin yarn to remaining sts at
center front.
ROW 26: purl.
ROW 27: k6, s1, k1, psso, k1.
Cont decs as set and work to
match first side.

Cuff

Using M, pick up and knit 34sts
around ankle. Work 24 rows in k1,
p1 rib. Change to C, knit 1 row.
Bind (cast) off.

Second bootee

Make second bootee to match.

FINISHING

Join heel seam, pin to heel end of
sole. Carefully pin upper to sole,
easing any excess around toe
area, and stitch into position
(see page 123). Weave in any
loose ends.

lacey leaf bootees
Pretty and nostalgic, these are lovely bootees for a baby girl. The lace edging complements the leaf pattern.

SIZE
To fit baby of 3–6 months

MATERIALS
Rowan dk wool
1¾oz (50g) ball of
 pink   1
1 pair of US 6 (4mm) needles
30in (76cm) of ribbon

BEFORE YOU START
Gauge (Tension)
22sts and 30 rows = 4in (10cm)
square over stockinette (stocking)
stitch using US 6 (4mm) needles.

Abbreviations
See page 126.

BASIC KNIT
Sole
Cast on 27sts and work as folls:
ROW 1 & ALT ROWS: knit.
ROW 2: *k1, inc, k10, inc* twice, k1.
ROW 4: *k1, inc, k12, inc* twice, k1.
ROW 6: *k1, inc, k14, inc* twice, k1.
ROW 8: *k1, inc, k16, inc* twice, k1.
ROW 10: *k1, inc, k18, inc* twice, k1. (47sts)

Upper
ROWS 11–19: knit.

Shape top of foot
ROW 1: k28, s1, k1, psso, turn.
ROW 2: s1, p9, p2tog, turn.
ROW 3: s1, k9, s1, k1, psso, turn.
ROWS 4–13: as rows 2–3 five times.
ROW 14: s1, p9, p2tog, turn. (33sts)
ROW 15: s1, k21.
ROW 16: purl across all sts.
ROW 17: knit.
ROW 18: purl.
ROW 19: make eyelets, *k1, yo, k2tog* to end.
ROW 20: knit.
ROW 21: purl.
ROW 22: knit.
ROW 23: p4, *k1, p5* four times, k1, p4.
ROW 24: k4, *p1, k5* four times, p1, k4.
ROW 25: p4, *yo, k1, yo, p5* four times, yo, k1, yo, p4.

ROW 26: k4, *p3, k5* four times, p3, k4.
ROW 27: p4, [*k1, yo* twice, k1, p5] four times, *k1, yo* twice, k1, p4.
ROW 28: k4, *p5, k5* four times, p5, k4.
ROW 29: p4, *k2, yo, k1, yo, k2, p5* four times, k2, yo, k1, yo, k2, p4.
ROW 30: k4, *p7, k5* four times, p7, k4
ROW 31: p4, *k2, s1, k2tog, psso, k2, p5* four times, k2, s1, k2tog, psso, k2, p4.
ROW 32: as row 28.
ROW 33: p4, *k1, s1, k2tog, psso, k1, p5* four times, k1, s1, k2tog, psso, k1, p4.
ROW 34: as row 26.
ROW 35: p4, *yb, s1, k2tog, psso, p5* four times, yb, s1, k2tog, psso, p4.
ROW 36: knit.
ROW 37: purl.
ROWS 38–39: knit.
ROW 40: purl.
ROW 41: k1, *yo, k2tog* to end.
◆◆
ROW 42: purl.
ROW 43: knit.
ROW 44: bind (cast) off loosely.

Second bootee
Make second bootee to match.

FINISHING
Join leg and underfoot seam.
Fold top of leg to inside at ◆◆
holes and slip stitch into position.
Weave in any loose ends.
Cut ribbon in half, thread
through eyelets and tie in bow
(see page 123).

tweed bobble slippers

Subtle tweed colors work well with this design, but you could try classic black and white for a pierrot look.

SIZE
To fit baby of 0–3 months

MATERIAL
Rowanspun dk
1¾oz (50g) balls each of
   violet (A)   1
   blue (B)   1
1 pair of US 3 (3¼mm) needles.

BEFORE YOU START
Gauge (Tension)
24sts and 32 rows = 4in (10cm) square using stockinette (stocking) stitch and US 3 (3¼mm) needles.

Abbreviations
mb = k1, yo, k1, yo, k1 into next st, turn, p5, turn, k5, turn, p2tog, p1, p2tog, turn, k3tog.
See also page 126.

BASIC KNIT
Sole
Using B, cast on 3sts, working in seed (moss) stitch, inc each end of rows 1, 3 and 5.
Cont in seed (moss) stitch until work measures 3¼in (8cm).
Dec each end of next and every alt row to 3sts.
Bind (cast) off.

Upper
Start at toe. Using A, cast on 5sts and work in stockinette (stocking) stitch. Shaping rows only given.
ROW 1: k1, inc in next 3sts, k1.
ROW 3: k1, inc in next 5sts, k2.
ROW 5: k3, inc in next 6sts, k4.
(19sts)
ROW 9: k9A, using B mb, k9A.
ROWS 13 & 17: as row 9.
ROW 21: k8, bind (cast) off 3sts, k8.
On 8sts
ROW 1: purl.
ROW 2: k1, s1, k1, psso, knit to end.
Repeat rows 1–2 twice more.
(5sts)
Work 9 more rows.
Bind (cast) off.
Rejoin yarn to remaining sts at center and work to match.
ROW 2: knit to last 3sts, k2tog, k1.

Second slipper
Make second slipper to match.

FINISHING
Join heel seam. Pin upper to sole, easing any fullness at toe, and stitch into position (see page 123). Weave in any loose ends.

harlequin bootees

Jaunty turned-up toes and colorful pom-poms make these ribbed cuff bootees fun as well as functional.

SIZE
To fit baby of 6–9 months

MATERIALS
Choose from:

❶ Red cuff, red bobble
Rowan designer dk wool:
1oz (25g) each of

blue (A)	1
red (B)	1
yellow (C)	1

2 red bobble

❷ Blue cuff, green bobble
Rowan designer dk wool:
1oz (25g) each of

red (A)	1
blue (B)	1
yellow (C)	1

2 green bobbles

❸ Red cuff, blue bobble
Rowan designer dk wool:
1oz (25g) each of

blue (A)	1
red (B)	1
yellow (C)	1

2 blue bobbles

❹ Blue cuff, red bobble
Rowan designer dk wool:
1oz (25g) each of

red (A)	1
blue (B)	1
yellow (C)	1

2 red bobbles

1 pair of US 3 (3¼mm) needles.

BEFORE YOU START
Gauge (Tension)
24sts and 32 rows = 4in (10cm) square over stockinette (stocking) stitch using US 3 (3¼mm) needles.

Abbreviations.
s2 = slip next 2sts purlwise.
See also page 126.

BASIC KNIT
First bootee
Sole
Using A, cast on 41sts.
ROW 1: *inc, k18, inc* twice, k1.
ROWS 2–3: knit.
ROW 4: *inc, k20, inc* twice, k1.
ROWS 5–6: knit.
ROW 7: *inc, k22, inc* twice, k1. (53sts)
ROW 8: knit, break A.
ROW 9: using C, knit.
ROW 10: purl.
ROW 11: k1, *yo, k2tog* to end.
ROW 12: purl.
ROWS 13–14: as rows 9 –10.
ROW 15: make hem, fold work at row of holes and knit together, 1 stitch from needle and 1 stitch from row 9, across row.
ROW 16: k2tog, k51, break C.

Sides
ROW 17: knit 26A, 26B.
ROW 18: using B, k24, inc, k1, yf, using A, inc, k25.
ROW 19: knit 27A, 27B.
ROW 20: using B, k25, inc, k1, yf, using A, inc, k26.
ROWS 21–28: inc as set. (64sts)
ROW 29: knit 32A, 16B, turn.
ROW 30: using B, s1, k13, inc, k1, yf, using A, inc, k15, turn.
ROW 31: s1, k16A, k13B, turn.
ROW 32: using B, s1, k10, inc, k1, yf, using A, inc, k12, turn.
ROW 33: s1, k13A, k10B, turn.
ROW 34: s1, k9B, yf, k10A, turn.
ROW 35: s1, k9A, k6B, turn.
ROW 36: s1, k5B, yf, k6A, turn.
ROW 37: s1, k5A, k2B, turn.
ROW 38: s1, k1B, yf, k2A, s1, turn. Break yarns.

Shape top
ROW 39: using C, k2tog, k2, s1, k1, psso, turn.
ROW 40: k4, s2, turn.
ROW 41: k3tog, k2, s1, k2tog, psso, turn.
ROW 42: k4, s2, turn.
ROWS 43–52: as rows 41–42 five times.
ROW 53: k1, k2tog, k2, s1, k1, psso, k1, turn.
ROW 54: k6, s1, turn.

❶

ROW 55: **k2tog, k4, s1, k1, psso, turn.**
ROW 56: **k6, s1, turn.**
ROWS 57–60: **as rows 55–56 twice.**
ROW 61: **k8, turn.**
ROW 62: **k8, yf, slip next 13sts, break C.** *(34sts)*

Shape ankle cuff

ROWS 1–4: **using B, knit.**
ROWS 5–32: **✳k1, p1✳ to end, break B.**
ROW 33: **using C, purl.**
ROW 34: **bind (cast) off loosely.**

Second bootee

Cast on and work rows 1–16 as for first bootee.
ROWS 17–38: **use B for A and A for B**
ROWS 39 TO END: **as for first bootee.**

FINISHING

Using a flat seam, join sole and back seam. Weave in any loose ends. Attach small bobble, obtainable at good haberdashery or craft shops. to toes (see page 123).

ribbon-tie bootees
These pink bootees are one of my favorite designs. With their simple shape and velvet ribbons, they stay on baby's feet and are stylish, too.

SIZE
To fit baby of 3–6 months

MATERIALS
Rowan dk wool
1¾oz (50g) ball of
    pink   1
1 pair of US 5 (3¾mm) needles
30in (76cm) of ribbon

BEFORE YOU START
Gauge (Tension)
24sts and 32 rows = 4in
(10cm) square over stockinette
(stocking) stitch using US 5
(3¾mm) needles.

Abbreviations
See page 126.

BASIC KNIT
Sole
Cast on 21sts and work in seed
(moss) stitch. Inc each end of
rows 2, 4 and 6. Work 3 rows.
Dec each end of rows 10, 12 and
14. Bind (cast) off.

Back and heel
Cast on 25sts and work 10 rows
in stockinette (stocking) stitch.
Change to k1, p1 rib and work
8 rows.
Change to stockinette (stocking)
stitch and work 13 rows, starting
with a purl row (A).
Bind (cast) off.

Front and toe
Cast on 3sts. Work in stockinette
(stocking) stitch. Shaping rows
only given.
ROW 1: inc, inc, k1.
ROW 3: inc in 4sts, k1. *(9sts)*
ROW 5: k1, inc in 2sts, k2, inc in
2sts, k2. *(13sts)*
ROW 7: k2, inc in 2sts, k4, inc in
2sts, k3. *(17sts)*
ROW 9: k3, inc in 2sts, k6, inc in
2sts, k4. *(21sts)*
ROW 11: k4, inc in 2sts, k8, inc in
2sts, k5. *(25sts)*
Cont to completion of row 22.
ROWS 23–24: seed (moss) stitch,
mark the 11th and 14th stitches (B1
and B2 in fig 4 on page 127).
ROW 25: bind (cast) off.

Second bootee
Make second bootee to match.

FINISHING
Refer to figs 3 and 4 on page 127.
Fold part A, see fig 3, of back and
heel to the outside and stitch
along the first row of stockinette
(stocking) stitch below the rib.
Join the front to the back by
seams B1-C1 and B2-C2, see figs
3 and 4. Join upper to sole. Cut
ribbon in half and thread through
cuff (see page 123).

slip-ons
These look fabulous in any shade and are so simple to knit that you can make a pair to match each of your baby's outfits.

SIZE
To fit baby of 0–3 months

MATERIALS
Rowan kid classic
1¾oz (50g) ball of either

dark blue	1
pale blue	1
cream	1
dark pink	1

1 pair of US 6 (4mm) needles

BEFORE YOU START
Gauge (Tension)
22sts and 40 rows = 4in (10cm) over garter stitch using US 6 (4mm) needles.

Abbreviations
See page 126.

BASIC KNIT
Sole
Cast on 14sts. Working in garter stitch, inc each end of rows 1, 3, 5 and 7. Dec each end of rows 9, 11, 13 and 15. *(14sts)*

(22sts)

Upper
ROW 16: cast on 5sts (for heel), k19. Inc beg rows (toe) 17, 19, 21 and 23. *(23 sts)*
ROW 24: bind (cast) off 10sts, knit to end.
ROWS 25–35: knit.
ROW 36: cast on 10sts, k23. Dec beg rows 37, 39, 41 and 43. *(19sts)*
Bind (cast) off.

Second slip-on
Make second shoe to match.

FINISHING
Join heel seam. Pin upper around sole, easing excess material around toe, and stitch into position (see page 123). Weave in any loose ends.

stripy socks This is a great design for using up oddments of yarns. Experiment with a variety of bold, bright colorways.

stripy socks cont

SIZE
To fit baby of 3–6 months

MATERIALS
Jaeger merino 4 ply
1¾oz (50g) ball each of
    dark pink (A)   1
    pale pink (B)   1
    cream (C)   1
4 double-ended US 2
(3mm) needles.

BEFORE YOU START
Gauge (Tension)
28sts and 38 rows = 4in (10cm)
square over stockinette (stocking)
stitch using US 2 (3mm) needles.

Abbreviations
See page 126.

BASIC KNIT
Note: place marker at beginning
of round.

Cuff
Using A, cast on 36sts (12, 12 and
12sts). Work 3 rounds in * k1, p1*
to end.
ROUNDS 4–5: using C, *k3, p1*
to end.
ROUNDS 6–7: using B, *k3, p1*
to end.
ROUNDS 8–9: using A, *k3, p1*
to end.
ROUNDS 10–27: as rounds 4–9
three times.

Start heel
Using A, k15, turn, leave
remaining sts on needles
for instep.
On 15sts, work 7 rows in
stockinette (stocking) stitch,
starting with a purl row.

Shape heel
ROW 1: k9, turn.
ROW 2: s1, p2, turn.
ROW 3: s1, k1, s1, k1, psso, k1, turn.
ROW 4: s1, p2, p2tog, p1, turn.
ROW 5: s1, k3, s1, k1, psso, k1, turn.
ROW 6: s1, p4, p2tog, p1, turn.
ROW 7: s1, k5, s1, k1, psso, turn.
ROW 8: s1, p6, p2tog, p1.
Break yarn.
Using A, pick up and knit 6sts
along heel, 9sts from needle,
6sts along heel, *p1, k3* five
times, from instep, move round
marker to here and last stitch to
left hand needle.

Cont as folls:
ROUND 1: using C, p2tog, k19,
p2tog, *k3, p1* four times, k3.
ROUND 2: using B, p2tog, k17,
p2tog, *k3, p1* four times, k3.
ROUND 3: using B, p2tog, k15,
p2tog, *k3, p1* four times, k3.
ROUND 4: using A, p2tog, k13,
p2tog, *k3, p1* four times, k3.
ROUND 5: using A, p1 k13, *p1,
k3* five times.
ROUNDS 6–25: as round 5, keeping
stripe pattern correct.
Break B and C.

Shape toe
Using A,
ROUND 1: knit to last stitch, slip
this stitch onto left hand needle to
be first stitch of next round.
ROUND 2: *k2tog, k13, s1, k1,
psso* twice.
ROUND 3: knit.
ROUND 4: *k2tog, k11, s1, k1,
psso* twice.
ROUND 5: knit.
ROUND 6: *k2tog, k9, s1, k1,
psso* twice.
ROUND 7: knit.
ROUND 8: bind (cast) off.

Second sock
Make second sock to match.

FINISHING
Join toe seam (see page 123).
Weave in any loose ends.

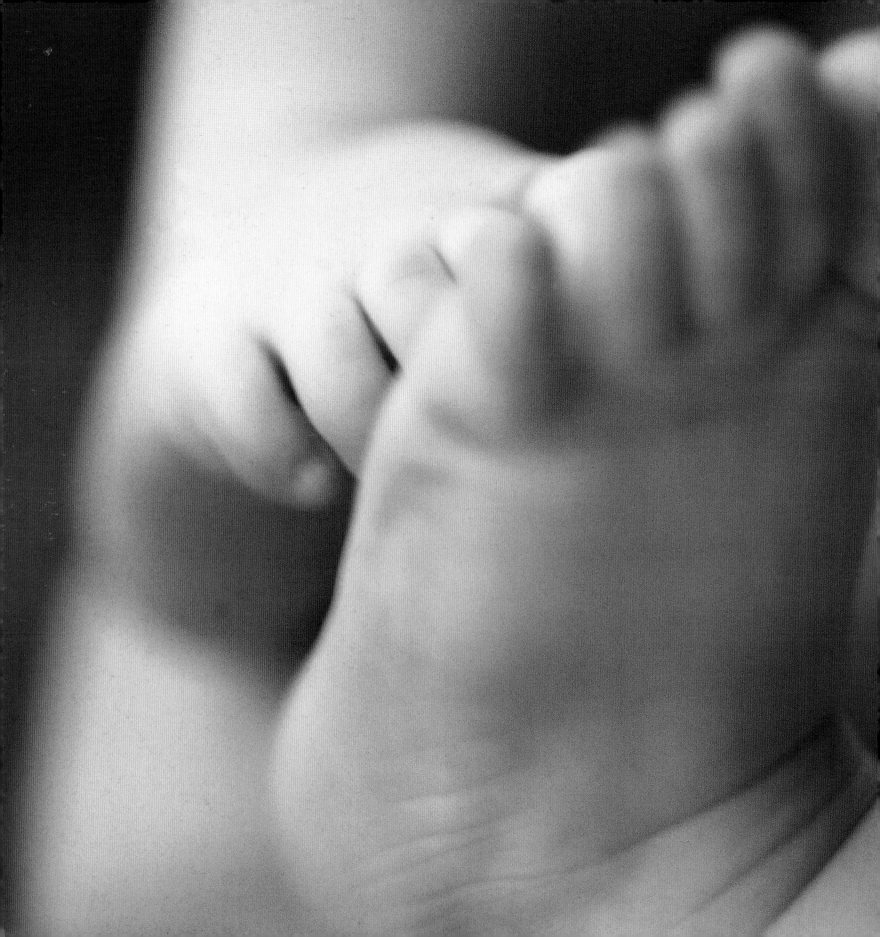

Knitting for babies

SAFETY

Most babies are fascinated by their own feet at some point in their lives and will happily grab anything put onto them and try to pull it off. Therefore you should take note of the following safety tips when knitting bootees.

- When adding ribbons or ties to bootees you should attach them to the back of the bootee with a stitch. This will ensure that the baby can't pull them off.
- All buttons should be firmly stitched on with strong thread and checked periodically to ensure that they remain securely fastened and that the baby cannot pull them off.
- If you are embellishing bootees with stitched on items, such as bells, pom-poms or motifs, stitch them on firmly and check them as for buttons.

WASHING

Most bootees can be hand washed in gentle washing powder or as instructed on the yarn ball bands. When washing the Jester Bootees on page 66 it is best to remove the bells before washing and stitch them on again afterwards. Check washing instructions on any store-bought embellishments.

YARNS

I have chosen a variety of yarns to make the bootees in this book. Most yarns these days are soft to touch, so they should not irritate a baby's delicate skin. However if your baby suffers from eczema it is a good idea to choose the cotton yarns to knit with rather than wool or synthetic yarns.

SEAMS

It is best to use a flat seam when sewing up bootees so that there is no ridge inside to rub against the skin. Lay the pieces out wrong-side up with the edges to be joined touching one another. Join the edges with oversewing stitches, matching the sides as you work. On roll-cuffed bootees you can reverse the seam on the top section of the cuff for a neat finish.

sizing small feet

When knitting bootees it is essential to check your gauge (tension) carefully (see page 126), as there is little room for error in such tiny patterns. If you want to change the size of a pattern, try knitting it on larger or smaller needles. The foot sizes here are an approximate guide.

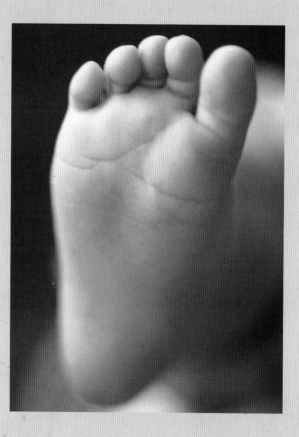

0–3 months	3¾in (9cm)
3–6 months	4in (10cm)
6–9 months	4½in (11.5cm)

pattern information

ABBREVIATIONS

The following abbreviations are those most commonly used in all the patterns. Where individual patterns have special abbreviations, these are explained at the beginning of the patterns. Where bound (cast) off stitches are given in the middle of a row, the last stitch of the bind (cast) off is always included in the instructions that follow.

alt = alternate
beg = beginning
C = contrast color
cont = continue
dec = decrease by knitting the next 2 stitches together
foll = following
inc = increase by knitting into the front and back of the next stitch
k = knit
k1, p1 rib = (on even number of sts) every row: *k1, p1* to end. = (on odd number of sts) row 1: *k1, p1* to last, k1. row 2: k1 *k1, p1* to end
k2tog = knit next 2 stitches together
k3tog = knit next 3 stitches together
M = main color
m1 = make stitch by picking up yarn before next stitch and knitting into the back of made loop
p = purl
p2tog = purl next 2 stitches together
p2togb = purl next 2 stitches together through back of loops
p3tog = purl next 3 stitches together
patt = pattern
psso = pass slipped stitch over
rem = remaining
s1 = slip next stitch

seed (moss) stitch = (on even number of sts) row 1: *k1, p1* to end. row 2: *p1, k1* to end = (on odd number of sts) every row: *k1, p1* to last st, k1
stockinette (stocking) stitch = row 1: knit, row 2: purl
st(s) = stitch(es)
tog = together
yb = yarn back
yf = yarn forward
yo = yarn around needle
** = repeat enclosed instructions the number of times indicated
( ) = brackets refer to larger size(s). Where only one figure is given it refers to all sizes

NEEDLE SIZES

This table shows the various international needle sizes.

Metric	British	American
2¾mm	12	2
3mm	11	3
3¼mm	10	3
3¾mm	9	5
4mm	8	6
4½mm	7	7
5mm	6	8

HOW TO DO A GAUGE (TENSION) SQUARE

Please check your own gauge (tension) before you start. Some people find that they need to use a smaller needle when knitting cotton. Cast on at least 30sts and work at least 40 rows. Measure only the sts given (e.g. 22sts by 28 rows) to check your gauge (tension). Remember that one stitch too many or too few over 4in (10cm) can spoil your work. If you have too many stitches, change to a larger needle, or if you have too few, change to a smaller size, and try again until the gauge (tension) square is correct. Note: yarns from different manufacturers may not knit to the gauge (tension) given.

COLOR KNITTING

Most of the multi-colored designs in this book are worked using the Fair Isle technique where the yarn is carried across the back of the work. However, a few designs use the intarsia method, which involves using separate balls of contrast colors, or shorter lengths wound around bobbins, but NOT carrying the main yarn across the back of the section. Twist the yarns around one another at the color change to avoid holes forming.

CARE INSTRUCTIONS

Steam your knitting lightly by using a warm iron over a damp cloth. Never let the iron come directly in contact with the knitting. Ease the knitting into shape, or block it out with pins until the steam has completely dried off. For washing instructions, see the yarn ball bands.

FINISHING SHEEP BOOTEES, PAGE 32

Front and toe – purl side is right side. Fold front in half lengthwise and join cast on edge, A to A, to make toe, see fig 2.
Back and heel – knit side is right side. Join back and heel section to front by stitching seams B1-C1 and B2-C2, see figs 1 and 2.
Join upper to sole.

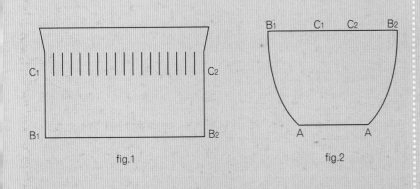

fig.1   fig.2

FINISHING RIBBON-TIE BOOTEES, PAGE 114

Fold part A, see fig 3, of back and heel to the outside and stitch along the first row of stockinette (stocking) stitch below the rib. Join the front to the back by seams B1-C1 and B2-C2, see figs 3 and 4.
Join upper to sole.

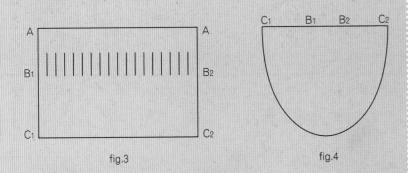

fig.3   fig.4

ENTRELAC

Use these diagrams in conjunction with the instructions to knit the Entrelac Socks on page 80.

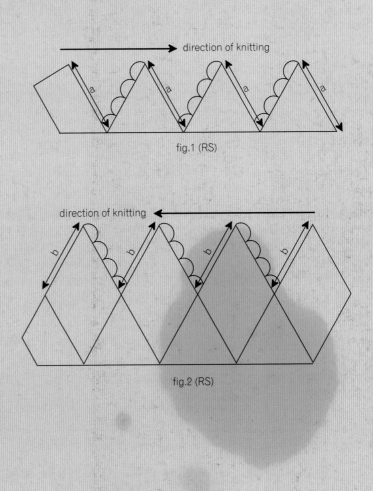

direction of knitting

fig.1 (RS)

direction of knitting

fig.2 (RS)

ACKNOWLEDGMENTS

Thanks to Eva for her expert pattern checking and for fitting this book into her busy schedule travelling the world. Thanks to Joey for his beautiful photographs. Thanks to Kate Haxell for all the fun we had on the photo shoots, for the delicious breakfasts to start our days and for making the book look the way it does. Thanks also to Kate Kirby for asking me to do this book, which has been a great joy to design items for. Thanks also to Amy, whose beautiful little toes show off some of the designs so well and who was such a happy baby to have around.

SUPPLIERS

Zoë Mellor can be contacted at: Toby Tiger, 15 Montpelier Place, Brighton, East Sussex, BN1 3BF.

Suppliers of Rowan yarns

UK
Rowan Yarns
Green Mill Lane
Holmfirth
West Yorkshire
HD7 1RW
Tel: 01484 681881
www.rowanyarns.co.uk

USA
165 Ledge Street
Nashua, NH 03060
Tel: 603 886 5041
www.westminsterfibers.com

Canada
Diamond Yarn
9697 St Laurent
Montreal
Quebec H3L 2N1
Tel: 514 388 6188

155 Martin Ross
Unit 3
Toronto
Ontario M3J 2L9
Tel: 416 736 6111
www,diamondyarn.com

Australia
Rowan at Sunspun
185 Canterbury Road
Canterbury
Victoria 3126
Tel: 03 9830 1609